SHIPWRECKS

SHIPWRECKS

CATHIE CUSH

MetroBooks

Dedication
—To Ed

MetroBooks

An Imprint of Friedman/Fairfax Publishers

Library of Congress Cataloging-in-Publication Data.

Cush, Cathie, 1957-
    Shipwrecks / Cathie Cush.
        p. cm.
    Includes bibliographical references and index.
    ISBN 1-56799-475-X
    1. Shipwrecks. I. Title.
G525.C964 1997
910.4'52—dc21   97-141

Editor: Celeste Sollod
Art Designer: Kevin Ullrich
Design/layout: Elan Studio
Photography Editor: Deidra Gorgos

Color separations by
Bright Arts Graphics (S) Pte Ltd
Printed in the United Kingdom by Butler & Tanner
  Limited

1 3 5 7 9 10 8 6 4 2

For bulk purchases and special sales, please contact:
Friedman/Fairfax Publishers
Attention: Sales Department
15 West 26th Street
New York, New York 10010
212/685-6610 Fax 212/685-1307

Visit our website:
http://www.metrobooks.com

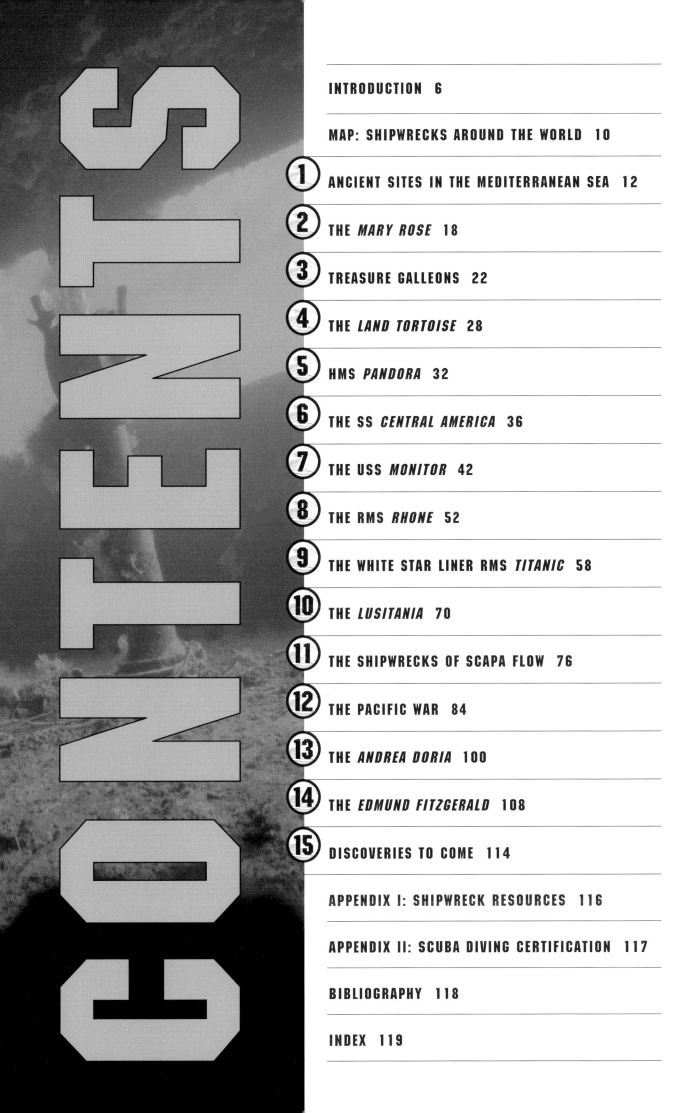

CONTENTS

INTRODUCTION 6

MAP: SHIPWRECKS AROUND THE WORLD 10

1 ANCIENT SITES IN THE MEDITERRANEAN SEA 12

2 THE *MARY ROSE* 18

3 TREASURE GALLEONS 22

4 THE *LAND TORTOISE* 28

5 HMS *PANDORA* 32

6 THE SS *CENTRAL AMERICA* 36

7 THE USS *MONITOR* 42

8 THE RMS *RHONE* 52

9 THE WHITE STAR LINER RMS *TITANIC* 58

10 THE *LUSITANIA* 70

11 THE SHIPWRECKS OF SCAPA FLOW 76

12 THE PACIFIC WAR 84

13 THE *ANDREA DORIA* 100

14 THE *EDMUND FITZGERALD* 108

15 DISCOVERIES TO COME 114

APPENDIX I: SHIPWRECK RESOURCES 116

APPENDIX II: SCUBA DIVING CERTIFICATION 117

BIBLIOGRAPHY 118

INDEX 119

INTRODUCTION

Toll for the queenly boat,
wrecked on the rocky shore!
Sea-weed is in her palace halls;
she rides the surge no more.

LYDIA HUNTLY SIGOURNEY (1791–1865)
"THE BELL OF THE ATLANTIC"

The title of this book is a little misleading. It claims to be about shipwrecks, but it is really about people. The wrecks themselves are jumbles of crumbling timbers, shells of rusting steel, piles of paraphernalia that no one would touch if they were lying by the side of the road. What fascinates most of us are the human stories that these hulks can conjure.

Sunken ships tell tales that touch universal themes: exploration, irony, fear and courage, life and death. The story only begins with the sinking. Those moments can be as gripping as anything Hollywood could imagine—such as when the captain of the doomed *Central America* asked a passenger aboard the last lifeboat to deliver a message to his wife, or when a crewman on the *Rhone* hung on to the stricken ship's mast awaiting rescue. The circumstances of the sinkings can be metaphors or morality tales, like that of the *Titanic*. Or, like the scuttling of the *Land Tortoise* in Lake George and the German fleet at Scapa Flow, they can be footnotes in history.

Settling on the bottom marks the beginning of a new chapter. It might be about determination, like Mel Fisher's obsessive search for the *Atocha*, or about the adventures of scuba divers such as Peter Gimbel. It could be about court battles for the right to visit the wreck—or even to obtain sole control over it. Oftentimes the ship becomes the storyteller, its cargo telling a maritime archaeologist like George Bass what the life of a trader might have been like thirty-five hundred years ago or how Henry VIII's navy fought a war. Seeing a shipwreck in its final resting place puts all those faces before you.

Not all shipwrecks hold gold and jewels or priceless antiquities, like the bounty found on the Spanish galleon *Atocha*. Still, each vessel is a sunken treasure in its own right. Each has a unique story to tell and, few tales rival the drama of a dying vessel. Perhaps that's why shipwrecks have so much power to capture the imagination.

I feel privileged to have visited many of the shipwrecks in this volume. In fact, it was hearing the story of a manned radar tower sinking in a storm as a Coast Guard cutter was racing to rescue its occupants that prompted me to learn to dive in the first place. That was in 1981. My first shipwreck dive took place on a nameless barge a few miles off Atlantic City, New Jersey. It wasn't very dramatic—just a boxy structure with collapsing iron hull plates. Yet, covered with peach- and ivory-colored *metridium* anemones and surrounded by schools of black sea bass, it was enough to whet my interest in shipwrecks. Since then, in waters around the world, I have seen wrecks as small as the eighteenth-century *bateaux* and as large as the liner *Andrea Doria*, as anonymous as an old car barge and as celebrated as the ironclad *Monitor*. The more stories I know about the wreck and the people associated with it, the more it touches my imagination.

I'm a sightseer, not an explorer. Over the years I have been fortunate to sit at the feet of those who know many more shipwrecks, and know them much more intimately, than I ever will, and to hear their tales. I wish that I could share all of their stories with you, and I hope that you will enjoy the ones chosen for this volume.

Cathie Cush

Above: The forces that sink ships range from war and weather to miscalculation and, sometimes, simple bad judgment. In light of the mortal consequences, these factors assume greater proportions. The sunken ships' remains call the human stories to mind. Left: After the USS *Arizona* sank in shallow water during the December 1941 raid on Pearl Harbor, dive teams entered the stricken ship's water-filled compartments to retrieve valuable parts of the battleship for installation on other vessels.

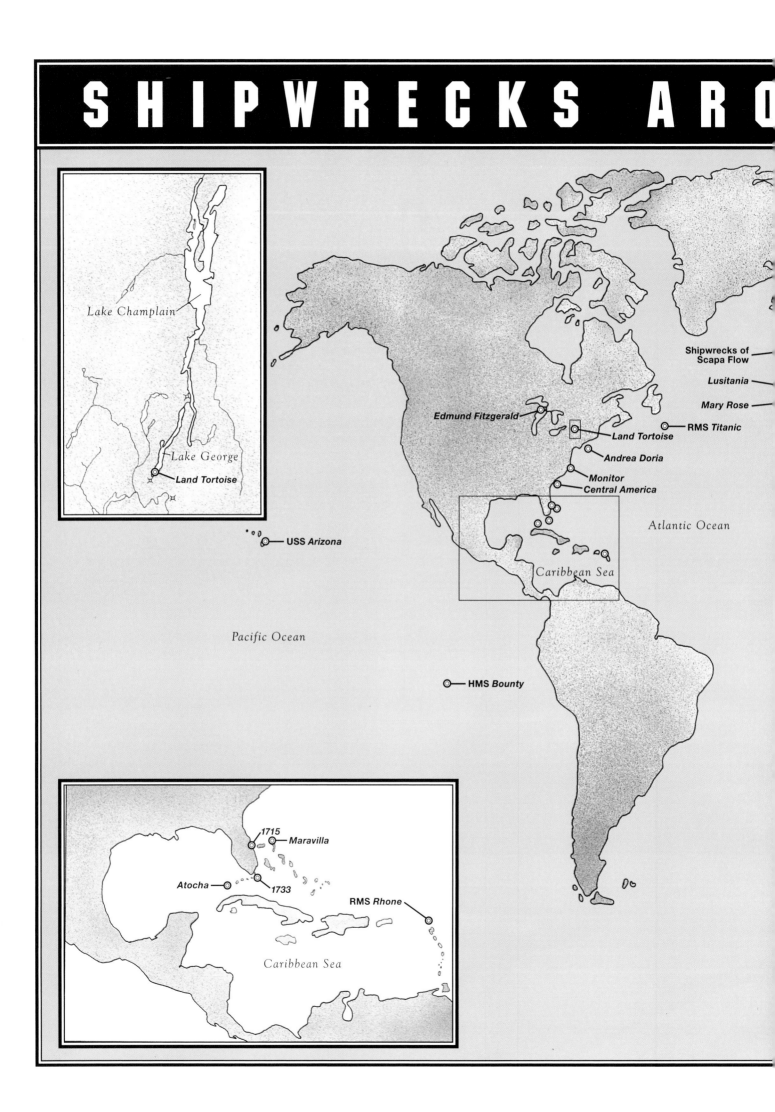

Lake Champlain

Lake George

Land Tortoise

Edmund Fitzgerald

Land Tortoise

Andrea Doria

Monitor

Central America

USS *Arizona*

Pacific Ocean

HMS *Bounty*

Shipwrecks of
Scapa Flow

Lusitania

Mary Rose

RMS Titanic

Atlantic Ocean

Caribbean Sea

1715 Maravilla

Atocha 1733

RMS *Rhone*

Caribbean Sea

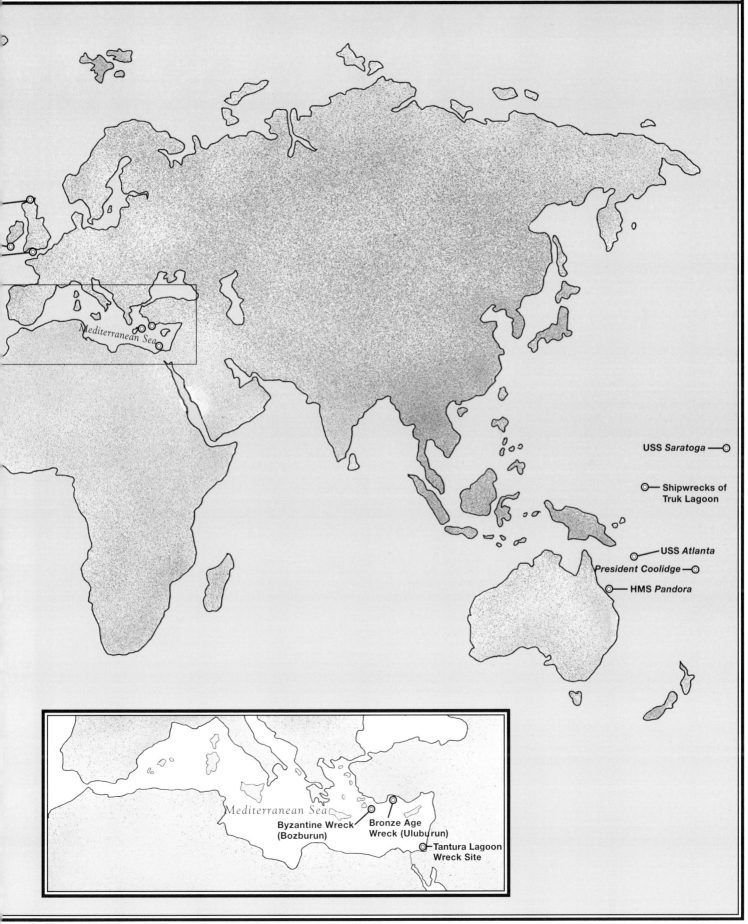

USS *Saratoga* ─◎

◎─ Shipwrecks of
Truk Lagoon

◎─ USS *Atlanta*
President Coolidge ─◎
HMS *Pandora* ─◎

Mediterranean Sea

Mediterranean Sea

Byzantine Wreck
(Bozburun)

Bronze Age
Wreck (Uluburun)

Tantura Lagoon
Wreck Site

CHAPTER ONE

ANCIENT SITES IN THE MEDITERRANEAN SEA

THE BRONZE-AGE WRECK AT ULUBURUN

One day in 1982 a Greek sponge diver named Mehmet Çakir slipped beneath the surface of the water and reached thirty-four hundred years into the past. Çakir found what looked like "metal biscuits with ears" at Uluburun, near Kas, Turkey. He reported his discovery to George F. Bass, Ph.D., an underwater archaeologist who was working on another project in the Mediterranean. It turns out that the "biscuits" were *amphorae* (two-handled jugs) from a shipwreck that would occupy Dr. Bass, Cemal Pulak, and their team from the Institute of Nautical Archaeology (INA) at Texas A&M University for the

Below: A Byzantine mosaic of the Roman port of Classis shows the type of ships sailed in the Mediterranean some fifteen hundred years ago. Right: Divers trained in archaeology use powerful underwater lights to examine a cargo of amphorae carried aboard an ancient vessel.

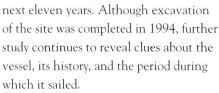

next eleven years. Although excavation of the site was completed in 1994, further study continues to reveal clues about the vessel, its history, and the period during which it sailed.

In addition to the amphorae, more than 150 of which were still intact and filled with resin, the ship carried ingots of copper, tin, and cobalt-blue glass; lumber, olives, and other goods. Pottery from the wreck dated the vessel to the fourteenth century B.C.—the Bronze Age—and other artifacts helped narrow down the date. A well-worn gold scarab, discovered in 1986, bore the name of the Egyptian Queen Nefertiti, and tree-ring counts of barkless cedar logs from the ship led the archaeologists to believe that the ship probably sank in the last quarter of the fourteenth century B.C. Further study may enable researchers to pinpoint the date more exactly; if so, they can cross-date pottery and other artifacts found at sites in the Aegean, Syria-Palestine, and Cyprus.

PERSONAL ITEMS AND PUZZLE PIECES

Two of the most intriguing questions about any shipwreck are who sailed the ship and from where did they come? At Uluburun, the archaeologists found twenty-four stone anchors of a type used by sailors from Cyprus and the eastern Mediterranean mainland, and they also found oil lamps from both Cyprus and Syria. The lamps, of two distinctly different shapes and materials, helped archaeologists piece together more of the puzzle. The nozzles of the Syrian lamps were charred, indicating that they had been used, while the Cypriot lamps were in pristine condition—which indicated that

Unique artifacts can often help archaeologists solve the puzzle of who sailed on a particular vessel. Other times, they only make the mystery more complex.

they were more likely cargo. In addition, most of the bowls, tools, weapons, and personal effects that the team excavated came from Syria or Palestine, giving researchers a closer indication of the vessel's home port. Personal items, including jewelry, a cloak pin, two Mycenaean swords, and two seals, have led the team to conclude that at least one, but probably two, wealthy merchants were aboard the ship when it went down. Other items raise more questions. For example, how did the merchants come to be carrying a ceremonial mace or scepter of a type found only near the Black Sea? Their fieldwork finished, the archaeologists will continue to study the salvaged artifacts for answers.

DIGGING AT DEPTH

At one time, excavating an archaeological site underwater was considered impractical and too expensive for the information it would yield. In the 1960s Bass and his mentor Dr. Peter Throckmorton proved the skeptics wrong, training archaeologists to use scuba equipment instead of costly surface-supplied air systems. At the Uluburun site Bass's team broke new ground and developed new techniques for underwater excavation.

Remains of the sixty-five-foot (20m) long wooden vessel at Uluburun lay on a steep slope between 150 and 190 feet (46 and 58m), making it the deepest wreck that the INA team had ever surveyed. At those depths, measuring and mapping the wreck and its artifacts was complicated both by the limited work time available and by the narcotic effects of breathing air, which contains oxygen and nitrogen, under pressure. An inert gas, nitrogen causes narcosis ("rapture of the deep") when breathed at high pressures. To minimize the risks of decompression sickness ("the bends") while increasing their work time, the INA divers breathed pure oxygen for several minutes before surfacing. This technique, which flushes excess nitrogen from the body, has since been widely adopted by other scientific and research divers seeking greater safety. Over the course of the excavation the divers made a total of 22,413 dives, representing more than sixty-six hundred hours underwater.

BACK TO BOZBURUN

When the Uluburun wreck was discovered George Bass was in the midst of surveying other Turkish sites. In fact, he had scheduled an excavation off the town of Bozburun on the southwest coast. However, further work on that site (found in 1973) was delayed until fieldwork at Uluburun was complete. Now teams of archaeologists and graduate students from Texas A&M, Instanbul, and Bilkent universities are exploring the site. The most prominent feature of Bozburun is a twenty-four-by-sixty-foot (7.3-by-18.2m) pile of amphorae on a sandy slope about 80 to 110 feet (24.3 to 33.4m) deep. An intact amphora has been dated to the ninth century.

For nautical archaeologists, the Bozburun wreck represents a unique opportunity to learn about a little-known time in Mediterranean maritime history. Differences between seventh- and eleventh-century sites indicate that many changes in shipbuilding, seafaring, and trade took place in the interim. And we do know that early in the ninth century, Moslem raiders took control of Sicily and Crete, putting the once-powerful Byzantine navy in a stranglehold. Unfortunately, however, archaeologists have had little opportunity to study vessels from the era. Only about a dozen wrecks from A.D. 750–1000 have been found in the Mediterranean, and none has been fully examined.

MYSTERY OFF ISRAEL'S MEDITERRANEAN COAST

Another site that has captured the INA's attention is Tantura Lagoon, just south of the ancient city of Dor on Israel's Mediterranean coastline. In fall 1994, as the Uluburun fieldwork was winding down, researchers from INA joined a team from the Recanati Center for Maritime Studies (CMS) at Haifa University to study timber fragments and artifacts at a site in the lagoon. What they have found may radically change what is known about ship construction before the seventh century.

A ship's water-soaked timbers are studied in place, then carefully preserved.

Shelley Wachsmann, of the University of Haifa, and colleague Kurt Raveh first identified the site on a routine dive following a storm in 1983. Touching something spongy, Wachsmann recognized the tip of a ship's frame protruding from the sand. The archaeologists gently fanned away some of the sand with their hands. On top of the planking, they uncovered intact jars and potsherds from the Byzantine period (A.D. 324–638). Further study two years later also revealed Byzantine artifacts.

A VIOLENT END?

When Wachsmann returned to the site nearly a decade later coastal construction and shifting sands in the lagoon forced the archaeologists to dig test trenches to relocate the hull, now buried six feet (1.8m) beneath the bottom. The teams found a swath of Byzantine artifacts some 180 feet (54.9m) long scattered across the floor of the lagoon. And instead of finding an intact hull, as they had expected, the archaeologists found scattered timbers indicating that the ship had been torn

apart. Many of the planks were charred; further study of the charring patterns will help researchers pinpoint when and why the fire took place.

Regardless of how it met its end, the ship was probably buried quickly after it sank, since many of its timbers were well preserved. As they had during previous excavations at the site, archaeologists again sent pieces of the wood for radiocarbon testing. The three samples they sent were dated to the fifth or sixth centuries, consistent with the pottery finds. Yet studies of the hull construction did not reveal the mortise-and-tenon joinery that the archaeologists thought they would find in a vessel of that period. Instead, the ship was built with frame-first construction techniques that were not believed to be used until at least the eleventh century—some five hundred years later.

It is possible that the ship was built at a later date, and that the Byzantine pottery washed over from another nearby wreck. The excavation of this site has uncovered artifacts from a wide chronological range, some dating back to 2000 B.C., so it is likely that the remains of

Above: Seals such as these, found at the site of the Bronze Age vessel at Uluburun, were used to mark the possessions of Egyptian royalty. The wreck also yielded a gold artifact traced to Queen Nefertiti. Left: Cemal Pulak, Ph.D., of the Institute of Nautical Archeology, examines exposed portions of the Uluburun wreck's hull. The small white tags mark mortise-and-tenon joints, used to fasten the timbers without nails.

several vessels lie in the immediate area. Even so, based on the radiocarbon testing, nautical historians may soon be able to amend the book on ancient shipbuilding.

CHAPTER TWO

THE MARY ROSE

SALVAGE AFTER FOUR CENTURIES

Cannons fired through the morning mist in celebration as thousands of people, including the Prince of Wales, watched as, after 437 years, a three hundred-foot (91.2m) crane lifted the fragile remains of the sixteenth-century warship *Mary Rose* from the bottom of the harbor at Portsmouth, England. The successful salvage was the culmination of nearly twenty years of painstaking research and excavation by volunteers from around the world. It was a marvel of engineering. But it was far from the first attempt to raise the vessel.

THE SINKING

The reign of Henry VIII was marked by numerous political conflicts between England and France. In October 1544 the English fleet was dis-

The flagship of Henry VIII's fleet, the *Mary Rose* was on the way to lead a defense against French invaders when she sank suddenly in Portsmouth Harbor.

patched to The Solent, between southern England and the Isle of Wight, to prevent the French from blocking the sea passage between Dover and Calais. Among the vessels was the *Mary Rose*, a swift warship with ninety-one cannons on her gun decks. She carried more than four hundred sailors and three hundred soldiers.

Built around 1510, the 130-foot (39.6-m), seven hundred-ton (635,600-kg) warship was carvel-built, which means it had oak planks that met flush at the seams, which allowed the inclusion of watertight gun ports. Unlike the converted merchant ships of its day, the four-masted *Mary Rose* was built for war, with complete gun decks and a full armament. She was one of the first ships able to fire a broadside.

On July 19, 1545, amidst an attack by some two hundred French ships, the *Mary Rose* suddenly listed hard to starboard. As onlookers, including the king, watched in horror, the vessel turned turtle and sank. Various eyewitness accounts place the blame on poor handling of the sails, too tight a turn, overcrowding, or lack of discipline among the crew. As the ship listed, water poured in through the open gun ports on the lower deck. Only a handful of the men aboard survived.

Immediately after the sinking, salvage attempts began. The *Mary Rose* was slung on cables between two large merchant ships in hopes that the rising tide would lift her and she could gradually be moved to shore. The attempt failed. Next the salvage crew tried to drag the wreck to shallower water. Again they were unsuccessful. Records show that in December 1545 the salvors were paid for their efforts.

THE REDISCOVERY

For nearly three centuries, the *Mary Rose* lay in the mud beneath Portsmouth harbor, a time capsule encased in silt and clay. She remained undisturbed until June 16, 1836 when a fisherman snagged his gear. Two brothers, John and Charles Deane, who had invented an early diving helmet, went to untangle the line. There, in forty feet (12.2m) of water about three-quarters of a mile (1.2km) offshore, they found timbers and a bronze cannon. They recovered several more guns and other artifacts before abandoning their work on the wreck some time after 1840.

THE AMATEUR AND THE ARCHAEOLOGIST

More than a century later the *Mary Rose* story caught the imagination of Alexander McKee, a diver with the British Sub-Aqua Club. In 1965 he persuaded Margaret Rule, a professional land-based archaeologist, to help him relocate the remains of the historic wreck, once again covered by silt and mud. After three years of fruitless searching they solicited the help of Harold "Doc" Edgerton of MIT, and his high-tech company EG&G. Using his recently developed sub-bottom sonar, which detected anomalies beneath the sea floor, Edgerton found the vessel.

For the next ten years McKee, Rule, and a group of volunteers known as "Mad Mac's Marauders" studied the wreck, which lay on its starboard side at a sixty-degree angle. After the sinking, the hull had trapped sediment; this burial helped preserve the vessel. The excavation's momentum built as the volunteers uncovered another gun and three port frames.

THE *MARY ROSE* TRUST

The non-profit *Mary Rose* Trust was established in 1979, with Great Britan's Prince Charles—himself a diver—as president. Under Rule's direction, a full-time salvage team of six plus some 180 volunteers worked over the next two years to recover seventeen thousand artifacts. Using airlifts, they raised longbows, arrows, and other weaponry, as well as more personal items, including a surgeon's chest and a backgammon set. It was the most complete complement of Tudor weaponry ever found in a single location.

The hull was raised on October 11, 1982. A 217-ton (197,036kg) frame, engineered specifically for the task, distributed the vessel's weight evenly in order to prevent damage from excess pressure on any single area. As McKee, Rule, Prince Charles, and the worldwide media watched, the giant Tog Mor crane lifted the intact portion of the hull and placed it inside a steel cradle that had

Wearing a protective respirator, a conservator applies chemicals to the ship's timbers in order to prevent the now-fragile wood from crumbling as it dries.

been set on the bottom of the harbor. The project cost $8 million.

The remains of the *Mary Rose* are still undergoing the long conservation process necessary to prevent her centuries-old timbers from drying out and crumbling to powder. Initially, this required that the hull be sprayed with chilled, fresh water. Now polyethylene glycol, a preservative, is being used to replace the water in the cells of the wood. This will take up to twenty years to complete.

Inside a special building, the hull sits upright, and portions have been strengthened with titanium supports. After the hull has been conserved, internal partitions and cabins will be replaced. Visitors to the *Mary Rose* Exhibition in Portsmouth can view the artifacts and remains of this sixteenth-century warship—the only vessel of its type on display in the world.

Top: At the *Mary Rose* exhibition, visitors can see the hull of the sixteenth-century warship while it undergoes a painstaking preservation process. Above: Ship's fittings were among the seventeen thousand artifacts recovered by volunteers before the hull was raised in 1982.

CHAPTER THREE

TREASURE GALLEONS

SPANISH RICHES REMAIN IN NEW WORLD WATERS

When the phone rang for Mel Fisher at Captain Tony's, a watering hole in the funky town of Key West, Florida, it was a call that the engineer-turned-entrepreneur had awaited for nearly twenty years. His office had excellent news.

"You can put the charts away," Fisher's son Kane reported to Treasure Salvors, Inc., headquarters. He was calling via ship-to-shore radio from aboard the salvage vessel *Dauntless*, moored some forty miles (64.4km) west of the island resort. "We found the *Atocha*."

"Today's the day," Fisher had said many times over the years as he sought a treasure with a reported value of $400 million. He chanted the mantra through frustration and even tragedy, and persevered long after others would have been discouraged. Today finally was The Day.

It was July 20, 1985.

In the mid-1960s, Fisher had set out to find the *Nuestra Señora de Atocha*, one of the many lost Spanish ships described in John Potter's classic, *The Treasure Diver's Guide*. Built in Cuba in 1620, the 550-ton (499,400kg), three-masted galleon was part of a fleet that carried the treasures of the New World to King Philip IV of Spain. Heavily laden with silver from the mines of Potosí in modern-day Bolivia, and gold from what is now Colombia, the *Atocha* set sail from Havana with twenty-seven other ships on September 4, 1622—too late in hurricane season to avoid stormy weather. On the fleet's second day out, disaster struck.

Built to carry both cargo and arms, galleons were the protectors of the treasure fleets. The bulky, square-rigged vessels featured large fore- and aftcastles on their upper decks, making them notoriously unstable in storms. Riding low in the water from the weight of her cargo, the *Atocha* was at the mercy of the wind. When her foremast snapped, she bobbed helplessly, striking a shallow reef that ripped the bottom out of her hull. Sinking slowly, she drifted into deeper water, her cargo dropping to the bottom. Before the storm was over, eight vessels would be lost, including the *Atocha* and her sister ship, the *Santa Margarita*. A month later, a second hurricane tore apart what was left of the *Atocha*'s exposed upper hull, scattering a trail of treasure over seven miles (11.2km). Only five of the 550 passengers aboard the *Atocha* survived. Those on the *Margarita* fared somewhat better; sixty-eight of 330 were rescued.

According to most accounts, the *Atocha*'s remains lay off Florida's Middle Keys, and that's where Fisher began his search. He originally planned to end his foray after 101 days, but when the dead-

Based on the original construction contract found in the Archive of the Indies, the drawing shows how the *Nuestra Señora de Atocha* may have looked.

line arrived, he couldn't relinquish his dream. In 1970, Fisher's long-time friend, Dr. Eugene Lyon, found a valuable clue to the ship's actual whereabouts while he was searching the Archives of the Indies in Seville, Spain. An expense report for a salvage attempt on the *Margarita* placed the galleons off the Marquesas Keys in the Gulf of Mexico. Armed with this information, Fisher moved his operation to Key West. Soon after, his crews began to turn up tantalizing evidence that they were on the right track. In 1971, they recovered an anchor and a gold chain. Two years later Fisher's divers found three silver bars that bore markings matching those listed in the *Atocha*'s

manifest. Two more years of searching yielded some of the bronze cannons that the ship carried.

TOUCHED BY TRAGEDY

The isolated finds weren't much, but they were enough to keep Fisher convinced that the crew was nearing "the big pile," the *Atocha*'s mother lode. They were enough to keep him pursuing the dream even when money was so tight that he couldn't pay his crew. To raise funds, Fisher developed a creative approach to limited partnerships, which drew the ire of the Securities and Exchange Commission. He sold shares in

Combining commercial salvage with the principles of archaeology, a treasure diver measures the flukes of a galleon's anchor before it is recovered.

the company for a year at a time; investors shared in whatever treasure, if any, was recovered during that period.

Fisher also faced ongoing legal battles with the state of Florida, which had claimed jurisdiction over the search site in 1970—and first pick of twenty-five percent of the treasure. Maritime attorney David Paul Horan argued—all the way to the U.S. Supreme Court—for Fisher's right to keep his finds. The battle

Encrusted with coral, a cannon blends into the reef and may have been difficult to spot, but its iron content was easily detected by a magnetometer towed behind the search vessel.

took seven years to win and cost $1.6 million in legal fees.

Some critics say that Fisher's financial woes contributed to the project's greatest loss—the death of Fisher's son Dirk, Dirk's wife Angel, and crewmember Rick Gage. The three drowned when the *Northwind*, a dilapidated Mississippi River tug that Treasure Salvors used as a salvage boat, capsized at sea in 1975. The only improvement that the company had made to the boat was the addition of "mailboxes"— large metal tubes that Fisher designed to clear away sand by channeling the prop wash in the desired direction. This sand-clearing technique now has Fisher embroiled in another legal battle—this time with the National Oceanic and Atmospheric Administration. According

to the federal agency, such salvage methods harm the coral and seagrass within the Florida Keys National Marine Sanctuary. Fisher contends that his operations may even encourage new coral growth and create new habitats in otherwise barren areas.

BOMBS AND BOUNTY

The divers did clear the seabed of items that had nothing to do with the *Atocha*. The search area had once been used for target practice by U.S. Navy pilots. More than a few bombs lay strewn about the bottom. Day after day, the crews removed depth charges, rockets, shrapnel, and miscellaneous trash. In between, a few coins here and there kept the search interesting.

The only event momentous enough to delay the *Atocha* search—even temporarily—was the discovery of a nearby concentration of artifacts, including ballast stones and silver coins. Recovery and study of several silver bars confirmed Fisher's hunch that the wreck was that

of *Atocha*'s sister ship, the *Margarita*. Although 350 silver bars and thousands of coins from the *Margarita*'s cargo had been salvaged successfully soon after her sinking, the divers spent most of the spring and summer of 1980 recovering gold and silver from the site.

PERSEVERANCE PAYS

As Fisher has pointed out in numerous interviews, "It's a big ocean." To help narrow the search area, treasure hunters use a device called a magnetometer, which detects changes in the Earth's magnetic field caused by deposits of metals such as iron. The salvors hope that locating cannons and iron anchors will lead them to the treasure. Generally, the magnetometer, or mag, is towed behind the boat. When it registers a "hit," divers are put in the water to investigate the target. A solid hit in February 1985 led to the discovery of a cannon northwest of where the crew had been working. By Memorial Day the new

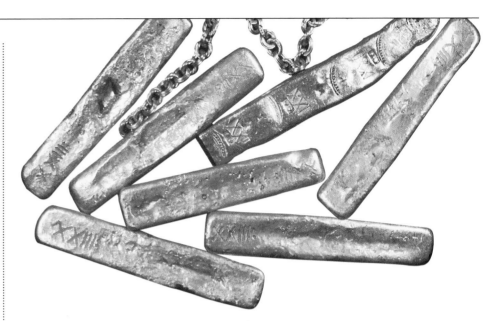

trail led the divers to thirteen gold bars, seven feet (2.1m) of gold chain, more than four hundred silver coins, and sixteen emeralds, worth as much as $4 million.

In the next two months the divers covered another two miles, but found little. Then on July 19 the adrenaline surged. From slightly off the search path, divers raised a barrel hoop encrusted with coins, and a ballast stone. The project's lead archaeologist, R. Duncan Mathewson III, had said that the heavy ballast—often musketballs—would be in the same area as the ship's more valuable cargo. Working until after dark, the divers found a cache of coins, barrel hoops, and potsherds.

The next morning, divers were in the water at dawn, investigating holes blown in the sand by the mailboxes. Using a metal detector in water fifty-five feet (16.8m) deep, Greg Wareham and Andy

Matroci, two of the approximately forty crewmembers, swam about fifty feet (15.2m) away from a hole where several others were working. The source of their signal was astounding: more than a thousand silver ingots stacked on the bottom

like cordwood. The two divers knew its significance immediately. Ironically, the mass of monofilament entangled in the silver bars told them that anglers had been fishing the site for years, never realizing the value of the "reef" beneath them.

The Atocha didn't disappoint. In the first week following the discovery of the mother lode, she yielded five hundred silver bars weighing up to one hundred pounds (45.4kg) each, as well as seven mahogany chests of silver coins and one full of gold bars. In fact, nearly a decade later, the Atocha and the Margarita were still giving up silver and emeralds—and inspiring anyone who ever dreamed of finding the riches that lay hidden beneath the blue waters of the sea.

Top and Above: Unlike silver, which oxidizes and turns to black when exposed to saltwater, gold retains its appearance no matter how long it is submerged. Spanish galleons carried gold bars bearing the stamp of the mint where they were cast, their value, and other identifying information.

FISHER'S FIRST TASTE OF TREASURE

When the Atocha's mother lode was discovered in 1985, it was the largest sunken treasure ever located. But it was not the first Spanish gold that Mel Fisher had ever found.

Fisher grew up in Gary, Indiana, and studied engineering in college. Following service in World War II, he worked as a carpenter in Chicago, later moving to Denver, then Tampa. Eventually Fisher followed his parents to California, where they

Salvage divers found a priceless emerald-studded gold cross among the *Atocha*'s treasures. In addition to fabulous jewelry and solid silver bars, the galleon yielded approximately three thousand loose emeralds—some as big as gumdrops.

claim rights to abandoned shipwrecks within their waters. As the first to salvage the vessels after they had been "abandoned" by the Spanish centuries ago, Fisher holds salvage rights to the wrecks under Admiralty Law. In turn, he can choose to sublet those rights.

For most, the search is a hobby that barely covers expenses. For others the effort is more fruitful. After working the wrecks for three years, in 1992 Stephen Shouppe's *Tequesta* brought in thirty-six gold doubloons; four hundred silver reales, or pieces of eight; a silver wedge, and other items. More recently, Bob and Margaret Weller and Chris James found a gold brooch with 170 diamonds, a gold butterfly with 144 diamonds, and other ornate jewelry.

MORE RICHES ARE RAISED

Between 1492 and 1789 approximately $60 billion in treasure passed through Havana on its way from the Orient and the New World to Spain. Contraband smuggled aboard the returning fleets could increase that figure by half again. Treasure hunters estimate that an eighth of the bounty may have been left at the bottom of the sea.

Since 1972 various salvors have worked the remains of *Nuestra Señora de las Maravillas* buried in the sand under thirty feet (9.1m) of water near the Little Bahamas Banks, about fifty miles (80.5km) north of Grand Bahama Island. With twice the *Atocha*'s cargo capacity, the three-masted galleon was carrying thirty to forty tons (27,240 to 36,320kg) of silver and gold when it left Havana in January 1656, part of a flotilla of seventeen. A few days out the ships hit fog. Two of the vessels collided. One of them, the *Maravilla*, broke in half and sank, carrying with her one of the most valuable treasures in the western hemisphere. The registered cargo alone has been valued at $1.6 billion. The

ran a chicken ranch, and he got involved in the fledgling sport of scuba diving. In the late 1950s he opened a dive shop in Redondo Beach and spent his free time searching streams for gold nuggets. Bitten by the gold bug, he moved his family to the east coast of Florida, where he planned to spend one year looking for treasure.

Less than a week before Fisher's self-imposed time limit was to expire, he and partner Kip Wagner found gold in Fort Pierce Bay. It came from one of ten ships wrecked between Fort Pierce and

Sebastian Inlet in a hurricane in 1715. Divers are still finding treasure from the 1715 Fleet; some fifty salvors have contracts with Fisher to search the area where he holds salvage leases. Traditionally, anyone can search for a ship that has been lost, provided that its original owners have "abandoned" it, or given up any attempts to salvage the vessel. Once the ship has been located and identified, the salvor is usually granted rights to the wreck and its contents—although federal legislation in the United States now allows states to figure does not include a three-foot-tall (.91m) solid gold Madonna and child that were said to have been aboard. In 1986 Marine Archaeological Research Ltd. received a permit to work the site and has since recovered precious stones, including a 49.5-carat and a 100.85-carat emerald, as well as gold and silver ingots and jewelry. Elsewhere in the Bahamas, a group of salvors from Minneapolis leased search rights to a thousand-square-mile (2,590-sq. km) area. An aerial magnetometer survey in 1995 yielded more than one hundred targets, which may be associated with twenty different wrecks. Only closer examination will determine which sites might be of any significance, whether archaeological or otherwise.

The Spanish galleons carried beautiful decorative objects made of gold and silver (right). The precious metals were also minted in gold *escudos* and the silver coins known as "pieces of eight." The links of the gold chain below were also used as money; their value was probably tied to the escudo.

CHAPTER FOUR

THE LAND TORTOISE

A UNIQUE IMAGE OF A UNIQUE VESSEL

The image unveiled for an audience of shipwreck enthusiasts gathered at Lake George, New York, in autumn 1994 was remarkable for two reasons. First, it showed the perfectly preserved remains of the oldest intact warship in the Western Hemisphere, which sank in the lake in 1758. Second, the photograph took more than 350 hours to develop.

Obviously no ordinary photograph, the image was a computerized photomosaic of a fifty-two-foot-long (15.8m) craft called the *Land Tortoise*. Unlike conventional photomosaics, which underwater archaeologists use to document wreck sites, the image was a seamless, undistorted, nearly three-dimensional representation of the vessel. It appeared as if the camera had captured the upper section of the wreck in a single shot—an impossibility considering the ship's size and the lake's limited visibility.

Known as a *radeau*, French for "raft," the flat-bottom *Land Tortoise* was built as a floating fortress in 1758. It was to be used by the British and provincial armies

In the limited visibility of Lake George, underwater photographers must shoot close-ups, like this view hole, which allowed soldiers to peer through the warship's hull.

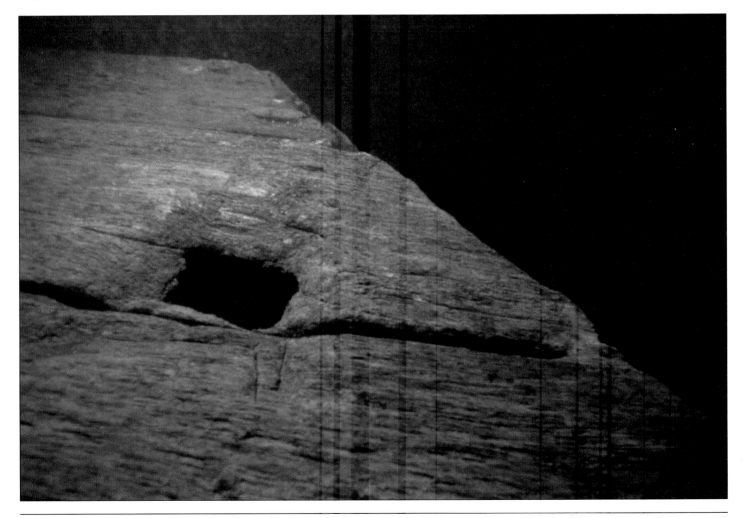

during the French and Indian War. The radeau had seven sides, the upper parts of which leaned inward over the deck to protect its occupants. Its seven gunports were staggered so that cannon crews would not interfere with each other during battle. Cannon ports on the bow and stern ensured that the ship was protected all around. It was powered by thirteen sets of oars.

According to historical records, two radeaux were launched on Lake George on October 20, 1758. Two days later, as the troops prepared to leave camp for the winter, the radeaux and numerous other vessels were filled with rocks and sunk in the lake for safe-keeping. The *Land Tortoise*, the larger of the two radeaux, was uncooperative and didn't slip beneath the surface until well after dark. By that time she apparently had drifted from the planned storage site. Although other vessels were raised the next spring, the *Land Tortoise* wasn't seen again for 232 years.

ADVENTURES IN ARCHAEOLOGY

On June 26, 1990, a group of shipwreck enthusiasts and dedicated amateur underwater archaeologists known as the Lake

Volunteer divers from Bateaux Below have surveyed and mapped several historic Lake George shipwrecks, including the *Land Tortoise* and seven French and Indian War–era bateau shipwrecks.

George Bateaux Research Team (now called Bateaux Below, Inc.) flew the prestigious Explorers' Club flag as they cruised the waters of the lake looking for French and Indian War–era wrecks. Using side-scan sonar, the team located an intact hull in 107 feet (32.6m) of water. It was the *Land Tortoise*, the only vessel of its type ever found. Over the next three years the

A floating gun battery, the fifty-two-foot (15.8-m) long *Land Tortoise* had seven gunports, each of which aimed in a different direction. A bulwark, or canopylike structure, would have protected the gunners from enemy fire. No cannons or artifacts were found on the wreck, which was sunk intentionally in 1758.

team surveyed the ship under the direction of archaeologists D.K. Abbass and Robert Cembrola, with a permit from the State of New York. The divers—including Joseph W. Zarzynski, Bob Benway, Vincent J. Capone, and Russell P. Bellico—focused on hull construction. They discovered

two mast steps, leading them to believe that the ship's builders planned to rig her (put sails on her) after raising her in the spring.

TRADITIONAL METHODS MEET NEW TECHNOLOGIES

In addition to mapping and still photography, survey techniques included videography done both by divers and by remotely operated vehicle. In order to generate the photomosaic, Benway took more than two hundred photographs, working along a flat plane and making sure that each image overlapped the pre-

vious one. Swimming along a measured grid over the wreck, he would shoot one frame, move forward slightly, then shoot the next. All told, he spent more than fifteen hours in the water.

When the photography was complete, the film was digitized and put on compact disc at the processing lab. Next, Kendrick McMahon, an Explorers' Club member, assembled the mosaic on a Macintosh computer, using image processing software to correct differences in lighting and color from one snapshot to the next. The end result of McMahon's more than 350 hours of labor was the image unveiled at an annual shipwreck conference hosted by Bateaux Below.

BEAUCOUPS DE BATEAUX

The group of volunteers who surveyed the radeau derived their name from a type of vessel that was far more common on Lake George. *Bateau* is French for "boat." Generally twenty-five to thirty-five feet (7.6 to 10.7m) long, bateaux were the workhorses of the waterways from the early 1700s until the War of 1812. Built of oak and pine, these flat-bottom boats carried nearly two dozen soldiers and enough provisions for a month. At one point during the French and Indian War, British General James Abercromby had nine hundred bateaux on the lake. In October 1758, 260 bateaux were sunk for safe-keeping along with the *Land Tortoise* and other vessels.

Discoveries of sunken bateaux in Lake George were reported as early as 1893. But it was the location of fourteen of the vessels by two teenage scuba divers in the summer of 1960 that put the wrecks in the archaeological limelight. Several bateaux were recovered and one was reconstructed for museum display. In the years that followed, archaeological examinations of bateaux took place at various sites around the lake, including Operation Bateaux in 1963–64 and a state police expedition in 1965. In 1987, under the guidance of *Atocha* archaeologist Duncan Mathewson, the Lake George Bateaux Research Team began a survey of seven bateaux offshore of the Wiawaka Holiday House. Their work continues with support from volunteers from New York and surrounding states.

In 1992 the Wiawaka Bateaux Site was listed on the State and National Registers of Historic Places. The following year the site was opened as one of New York State's first two Submerged Heritage Preserves. The other, the *Forward*, is in Lake George as well. In 1994 the *Land Tortoise* was also opened as a Submerged Heritage Preserve. The sites are marked by buoys, and the New York State Department of Environmental Conservation offers literature about their historic value. The designation creates an underwater museum and provides controlled access to the site by recreational divers. In 1995, the *Land Tortoise* was listed on the State and National Registers, and may be eligible for designation as a National Historic Landmark—a status attained by only four other shipwrecks: the *Utah*, the *Monitor*, the USS *Arizona*, and the Civil War Union warship *Maple Leaf*.

A thirty-four-foot (10.4m) long bateau recovered in the 1960s was one of several such vessels in use on Lake George in the eighteenth century. This one is on display at the Adirondack Museum. Seven more lie within a Submerged Heritage Preserve.

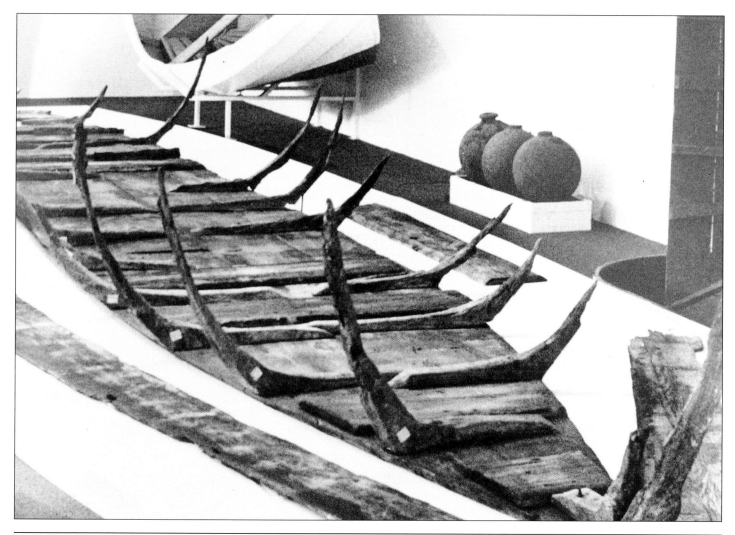

CHAPTER FIVE

HMS PANDORA

THE SHIP SENT TO BRING BACK THE BOUNTY MUTINEERS

The tale of the HMS *Pandora* begins with that of another ship: the HMS *Bounty*.

Lt. William Bligh sailed the HMS *Bounty* out of Portsmouth, England on December 27, 1787 with an excellent record of service. When he returned to England in July 1789 he was welcomed as a hero. In between, he had some problems.

Bligh's mission was to bring breadfruit trees from the Pacific to the West Indies, where they would be planted to feed the slave population. Along with a gardener, the gardener's assistant, and a crew of forty-seven, Bligh sailed the *Bounty*, which had been refitted as a floating greenhouse, to Tahiti. Although Bligh was the only commissioned officer aboard, his second-in-command was his friend Fletcher Christian.

TROUBLE IN PARADISE

The ten-month journey passed without major incident, despite low morale due to cramped quarters, strict discipline, and the captain's changeable moods. The *Bounty* arrived in Tahiti in October, where she was anchored for the next five months. Bligh stayed aboard the ship, relaxing his rules and allowing his crew to remain ashore. Many of the men, including Christian, fell in love with the simple island life—and the Tahitian women. They left the island on April 4, 1789, with heavy hearts.

Tension built on the *Bounty*. Bligh became stricter, the crew more surly. On April 28, Christian led a bloodless mutiny, putting Bligh and nineteen loyalists on a twenty-three-foot (7-m) raft that Christian had built for his own escape. Using only a chronometer for navigation, Bligh crossed 3,618 nautical miles of ocean to reach Timor in present-day Indonesia, where he was rescued and returned home.

THE *BOUNTY* BURNS

Under Christian's command, the *Bounty* returned to Tahiti. Some of the mutineers remained on the island. Christian and eight other crew members, along with a dozen Tahitian women, sailed on until they reached remote Pitcairn Island, where they established a settlement. They stripped the *Bounty* and burned her. The mutineers had no further contact with European civilization until 1808, when a whaling ship stopped at the island. In 1975, Luis Marden, a journalist with *National Geographic*, journeyed to Pitcairn, where the mutineers' descendants thrive. In Bounty Bay he found a ballast pile and a brass oarlock bearing the Royal Navy insignia.

THE FLOATING PRISON

Upon Bligh's return to England, the twenty-four-gun frigate *Pandora* under the command of Captain Edward Edwards was sent in search of the mutineers. Setting sail in November 1790, *Pandora* reached Tahiti five months later.

(Apparently, the *Pandora* had fewer delays on the journey than the *Bounty* did.) The fourteen mutineers who had remained on Tahiti were arrested and placed in irons inside a cramped cell known as Pandora's Box, on the frigate's quarter-deck. For the next several months, Edwards searched the South Pacific in vain for Christian. Finally he sailed west for England, planning to pass through the Torres Strait between northern Australia and New Guinea.

Lt. William Bligh and his supporters were set adrift in the vast South Pacific when a rebellious crew decided to remain in Tahiti rather than return to England with the cargo of breadfruit trees they had collected. Upon Bligh's eventual return, English officials sent Capt. Edward Edwards and the HMS *Pandora* to find and arrest the *Bounty* mutineers.

a telescope, a surgeon's chest, ivory syringes, and a working pocket watch. Ceramic jars were found intact. Prisoners' leg irons are poignant reminders of the *Pandora*'s purpose. Recent excavations have concentrated in the stern, where the officers' cabins and storerooms were located. By recording exactly where each item was found before bringing it to the surface for conservation, archaeologists hope to be able to match many of the artifacts with their individual owners.

SLOW GOING

Assuming adequate funding, the *Pandora* excavation is expected to continue into the next century. Strong currents and turbulent weather limit the work season to about six weeks of the year. Most of the lower hull is buried beneath an estimated 1,104 cubic yards (844.6 cubic m) of sand, which must be removed gently so as not to disturb the context in which the artifacts are found.

In addition to keeping artifacts in place, the sand also protected the wreck by shielding it from marine microorganisms. Recent microbiological testing by the University of Queensland shows higher levels of bacteria, fungi, and other microorganisms in the immediate vicinity of the wreck than are found several yards away. Even though those working the site are careful to replace disturbed sediments, the copper-lined English oak planks of *Pandora*'s hull are deteriorating as fodder for microscopic creatures in the sea.

Above: A skilled seaman who had explored the Pacific with Capt. James Cook, Lt. William Bligh was in command of the *Bounty* in 1787, when he was sent on a voyage to Tahiti that ended in mutiny. *Pandora* sought the mutineers. Right: The story of the *Bounty* mutiny continues to be told and retold in books and movies and to be portrayed in paintings, such as this watercolor by Cornelius deVries. The end of the *Bounty* story—the tragic tale of the *Pandora*'s loss and its discovery nearly two centuries later—is less well known.

On August 29, 1791, *Pandora* struck a reef, tearing off her rudder. The crew threw her cannons overboard to lighten the load, but the frigate drifted aimlessly, taking on water. At dawn the captain gave the order to abandon ship. Most of the crew followed the order quickly, leaving personal possessions behind and climbing aboard one of the small boats used for going ashore. Four of the prisoners and thirty-one crew members did not escape. The survivors reached Timor and eventually returned to England.

THE SEARCH FOR THE SEEKER

In the 1970s, the search for the *Pandora* began. Two underwater photographers, Ben Cropp and Steve Domm, spent five years looking for the remains of the frigate. They were aided by a Royal Australian Air Force plane equipped with a magnetometer for use in detecting submarines. In 1977, they spotted a target on the outer Great Barrier Reef, about sixty nautical miles east of the northern tip of Australia's Cape York Peninsula. When the divers went to investigate, in 110 feet (33.5m) of water, they found what they had been seeking.

The wreck was immediately declared a national monument. A survey wasn't begun until six years later after the Queensland Museum in Brisbane agreed to take responsibility for the site. Since then numerous archaeological expeditions have been mounted to survey the site and study the tools, weapons, and personal items among the wreckage. The hull's outline is visible, as are an iron anchor, coral-encrusted cannon, and the ship's galley stove.

Some of the more intriguing personal objects that have been recovered include

CHAPTER SIX

THE SS CENTRAL AMERICA

THE HIGH-TECH SEARCH FOR AMERICA'S RICHEST SUNKEN TREASURE

When the SS *Central America* sank in a hurricane in 1857, she carried the United States economy with her, and headlines screamed of the tragedy for weeks. Eventually the tale of the sunken paddlewheeler was replaced by more pressing stories. Policy-holders were paid, and the wreck was virtually forgotten. Then three men from Ohio using homemade—albeit highly sophisticated—equipment found the ship's cargo of gold. Suddenly, the *Central America* was back in the news.

THE LUXURY LINER OF THE FORTY-NINERS

The *Central America* left Havana harbor early on the morning of September 8, 1857, having arrived the prior evening. The 272-foot (82.9m) wooden sidewheel steamship was one of two that made regular runs from Panama to New York, often carrying successful prospectors from California who boarded in Panama. On this, her forty-fourth voyage, the *Central America* carried about 580 passengers and more than a hundred

crew members. She was laden with several tons of gold bars, freshly minted U.S. currency, and privately cast coins. New York banks eagerly awaited the ship's arrival, counting on the influx of gold to stave off an economic downturn that loomed on the horizon.

Traveling northward with the Gulf Stream, the ship hit the leading edge of a hurricane on the evening of September 9. The gale whipped the waves until they seemed to the passengers as tall as buildings. The winds shredded the sails, and water washed over the decks.

Within forty-eight hours the situation was dire. Battered by waves, the *Central America* took on water in her lower holds; the flooding extinguished the boilers that powered her engine. Without power, the bilge pumps failed. Crew and passengers tried in vain to bail out the ship.

RAISING HOPE FOR RESCUE

Commander William Lewis Herndon had ordered the flag flown upside down to signal the ship's distress. The brig *Marine*, herself battered by the storm but not as badly damaged as the *Central America*, responded to the stricken vessel. On the afternoon of September 12, all women and children, along with some male passengers—about ninety people in all—were placed aboard three lifeboats. Just before the last boat left, Herndon entrusted his gold watch and chain to one of the passengers, Theodore Payne, asking him to carry it to his wife. The captain started to give Payne a message for her as well, but only got a few words out before he was overcome with emotion. He waited a moment, composed himself, and once again began issuing orders.

Left: The sinking of the steamer *Central America* was front-page news, partially due to the great loss of life, and partially because she was carrying a cargo of gold. Above: Commander William Herndon was forty-four years old when he went down with his ship.

Manning the lifeboats, crew from the *Central America* rowed for more than two hours in the heavy seas before reaching the haven of the waiting *Marine*. The rescuers made as many trips as possible,

but by nightfall they could do little more than helplessly watch the stricken steamer's lights. At ten minutes before eight o'clock, Herndon fired three rockets, indicating that the sinking was

imminent. Those still on board the dying steamer donned lifejackets. Many grabbed doorways and other objects that might serve as rafts; others stood on deck, ridding themselves of pouches of gold that might weigh them down. Less than twenty minutes later, the paddle-wheeler slipped, stern first, beneath the sea. Grief was palpable as those on the *Marine* watched the *Central America's* lights disappear.

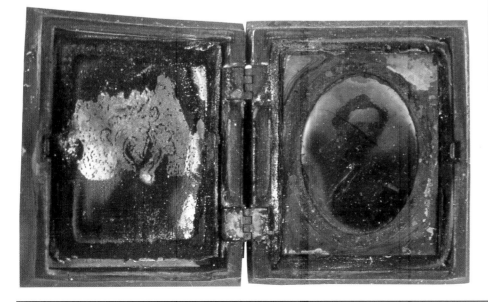

Above and Left: Of the nearly six hundred passengers and more than one hundred crew members aboard the Central America, only about 170 were saved. More than 120 years later, personal artifacts such as steamer trunks and picture frames found at the site serve as poignant reminders of the lives that were lost.

The bark, or sailing ship, *Ellen* picked up some fifty men from the water. Nine days later, three more survivors were found on a raft four hundred miles (643.6km) northeast of where the ship sank. More than four hundred of the six hundred people on board died in what was at the time America's greatest maritime disaster. William Lewis Herndon went down with his ship. The loss of the gold ignited the Panic of 1857.

Dishes lie scattered in the deep-sea sediment near one of the few remaining timbers from the *Central America*. Some eight thousand feet (2,438.4m) below the surface, the wreckage sheltered unusual marine life in abundance.

TECHNOLOGY TO TOUCH THE BOTTOM OF THE SEA

In 1981 Thomas Thompson, an ocean engineer with a background in deep-sea mining, formed the Columbus-America Discovery Group, Inc. to locate the *Central America* and salvage her cargo. His partners in the venture were geologist Robert Evans and journalist Barry Schatz. With backing from 166 investors, the group raised $10 million to get the project going.

Eyewitness accounts of the sinking were plentiful in newspaper archives. In addition to the anecdotal accounts, the team researched historical wind and tide information and used it to generate computer models of the storm and the ship's possible movements. Based on the results, they narrowed their search area to a mere fourteen hundred square miles (3626 sq. km) along the Blake Ridge, about 200 miles (320km) off South Carolina. Using side-scan sonar they swept the bottom of the ocean. They used a structured search pattern indicated by computer software developed especially for deep-sea search and recovery—and the *Central America* was certainly deep. In 1987 a lump of coal

THE ARMS OF NEMO

brought up from the bottom told the salvors that they had found a steamship; the following season, recovery of the ship's bell confirmed the identify of the Central America. The wreckage was found in more than eight thousand feet (2,438.4m) of water—making it thirty times deeper than any other archaeological project undertaken previously.

A mile and a half (2.4km) beneath the surface, a manned recovery was out of the question. Instead, the team relied on a remotely operated vehicle (ROV) of their own design. Equipped with video cameras, ROVs are commonly used for undersea observation. Columbus-America's NEMO, however, was far more versatile than most. With a variety of interchangeable modules, NEMO could be configured to accomplish an array of tasks, including videotaped surveying, probing, excavating, and lifting. The 12,000-pound (5,448kg) unit was capable of raising thousand-pound (454kg) anchors—and was equally adept at lifting

delicate items without causing damage. One highly specialized module covered coins with a polymer coating, picking up the entire mass after the silicone congealed. The team's salvage ship, R/V (Research Vessel) *Arctic Discoverer*, remained anchored over the site for forty days, bringing up more than half of the three-ton commericial shipment (3,178kg) of gold.

Treasure wasn't all the salvors found. Little remained of the wooden vessel itself, but living among the remains of the cargo was an abundance of marine creatures—some of which had never before been seen. Among the wood-boring clams, glass sponges, gorgonian corals, feather stars, and other life forms found at the wreck site, at least eleven were new to science. Biological specimens and sediment samples were taken from the site and shared with researchers.

GOLD FEVER CAUSES LEGAL FIGHTS

The trouble started on August 27, 1989, when Columbus-America Discovery Group sailed into port at Norfolk, Virginia with a cargo of recovered gold. Thirty-nine insurance companies and assorted other parties laid claim to the treasure. The court battles continued for years. All the while, the treasure sat in custody of the U.S. Marshals Service.

Columbia University claimed that its researchers located the wreck in 1984, but never positively identified it. Two other treasure hunters, Texas oilman Jack Grimm and Harry G. John, an heir to the Miller Brewing Co., funded Columbia's search and felt they were entitled to the treasure. An order of monks claimed to have been given John's rights to the treasure, which they sold back to him for ten dollars. The insurance companies, because they had paid off claims at the time of the sinking, believed that the wreck and its contents belonged to them.

NEW LEGAL GROUND

The case was heard first in U.S. District Court in 1990. Citing traditional admiralty law, Judge Richard B. Kellam ruled that the insurers had abandoned the wreck by not attempting to salvage it themselves, and therefore relinquished their rights. The judge rejected their claims along with Grimm's, John's, and the other insurance companies'. In granting salvage rights to the Columbus-America Discovery Group, the court set several precedents. The deci-

Discovery of the *Central America*'s treasures sparked custody battles that stayed in court for years.

sion marked the first time that a private interest had been granted rights to the deep ocean. It was also the first time that a salvor had used remote technology, rather than physical contact, to establish claim to a wreck site.

Legal wrangling continued for years. The Fourth Circuit Court of Appeals reversed Kellam's decision in 1992. After the Supreme Court later declined to hear the case, the parties found themselves once

again before Judge Kellam. On November 18, 1993, Kellam awarded the Columbus-America Discovery Group, Inc. ninety percent of the treasure they salvaged from the SS *Central America*. In later proceedings, Columbus-America was awarded in excess of 92 percent of the insured gold and 100 percent of all other gold and artifacts. Estimates of the value the gold bullion range from $21 million to more than $450 million.

CHAPTER SEVEN

THE USS MONITOR

IRONCLAD WARSHIPS COME OF AGE

Two odd and ungainly looking adversaries faced each other for the first—and last—time on a sunny March morning in 1862. The now-historic clash between the two ironclad warships on the Virginia waterway known as Hampton Roads may have changed the course of the American Civil War. The battle between the USS *Monitor* and the CSS *Virginia*, also known as the *Merrimack*, certainly marked a new era in maritime warfare.

BIRTH OF A NEW KIND OF BATTLESHIP

In spring 1861, anticipating the Confederate takeover of Norfolk, Virginia, Washington gave orders to burn any ships and supplies that could not be removed from the Navy Yard. Among the injured ships was the wooden steam frigate USS *Merrimack*. It was burned, but not destroyed. Despite the Union's efforts, the *Merrimack* fell into Confederate hands, although in a manner no one had foreseen. She would be rebuilt, her vulnerable wooden sides covered with iron that would stop, or at least slow, any cannonballs or explosive shells fired at her. Rechristened the CSS *Virginia*, she was the Confederacy's best hope for breaking up the Union blockade of the Chesapeake Bay, which prevented the shipment of food and arms to Southern ports.

In the meantime, the Union learned of the *Merrimack*'s fate. With nightmare visions of the *Virginia* sailing up the Potomac and shelling Washington, the Union responded with orders to develop an ironclad vessel of its own. The contract for the design was awarded to John Ericsson, a Swedish-American engineer, and was carried out at a shipyard in Brooklyn, New York. The ship Ericsson designed was 172 feet (52.4m) long and about forty feet (12.2m) wide, with only about a foot (30.5cm) of freeboard above the waterline, so it presented a very small target. Around the hull was an armor belt of eight-inch-thick (20.3cm) iron. The ship drew only twelve feet (3.6m) of water, enabling her to navigate shallow areas, although awkward rudder placement sometimes made her difficult to steer.

Atop the low-profile hull sat a revolving gun turret, about twenty feet (6.1m) in diameter and nine feet (2.7m) high. An escape hatch on its roof offered access to the ship. The turret, too, was made of iron. Inside were two eleven-inch (24.6cm) Dahlgren cannons, each weighing more than eight tons (7,264kg). With this unique feature, the vessel looked to some like "a tin can on a shingle" or "a cheesebox on a raft."

Numerous artists have portrayed the historic Civil War battle between the *Monitor* and the *Merrimack*, renamed the CCS *Virginia*. Despite fierce fighting and claims of victory on both sides, the battle ended in a draw.

The revolving gun turret, or Ericsson's Battery, was a first, and so were many other features on the novel vessel. The ship was powered by a new type of steam engine, and boasted the first marine flush toilets. At Ericsson's request, the ironclad was christened USS *Monitor* in hopes that she would "check and control" the Confederate threat. In February 1862 she was sent to Norfolk.

CLASH OF THE TITANS

Early morning fog covered the Hampton Roads area of the Chesapeake as the sun rose on March 9, 1862. Aboard the *Virginia* the crews were jubilant. The day before, they had enjoyed a decisive victory, ramming the Union's USS *Cumberland* while cannonballs bounced almost harmlessly off the ironclad's seemingly invincible hull. Despite their

vessel's mortal wound, which had only cost the *Virginia* a battering ram, the crew of the *Cumberland* refused to surrender, and more than a hundred Union soldiers were lost when she sank. The *Virginia* then turned to the USS *Congress*, firing exploding shells at the Union ship for an hour until the captain and crew surrendered. For the first time, the Confederacy saw the possibility of breaking the blockade.

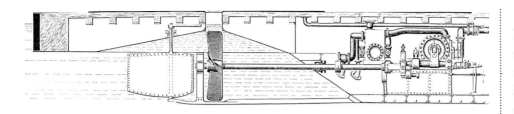

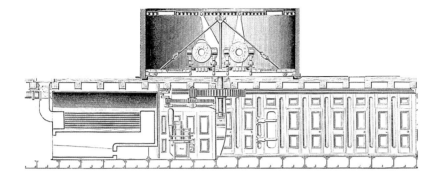

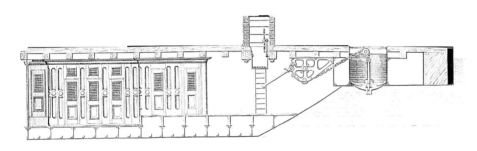

By eight in the morning the fog had lifted. The *Virginia* moved down the Elizabeth River and into the Bay, ready to attack and destroy the USS *Minnesota*, one of the Union's largest and most well-armed vessels, which sat stranded on a sandbar. As the *Virginia* approached, the *Monitor* appeared from behind the *Minnesota*. Hundreds of spectators lined the shores to watch the

Left: Cross-sections along the *Monitor*'s center line show the ironclad vessel's cramped interior spaces including, from top, the rudder, propeller, and propeller shaft in the aft section; living quarters and the famous gun turret in the central section; and additional quarters and a hatchway in the forward section. Below: An etching from *Battles and Leaders of the Civil War* (1984) shows the encounter between the two vessels at close range. Following a battle that lasted for hours, neither side could claim a decisive victory—although both did.

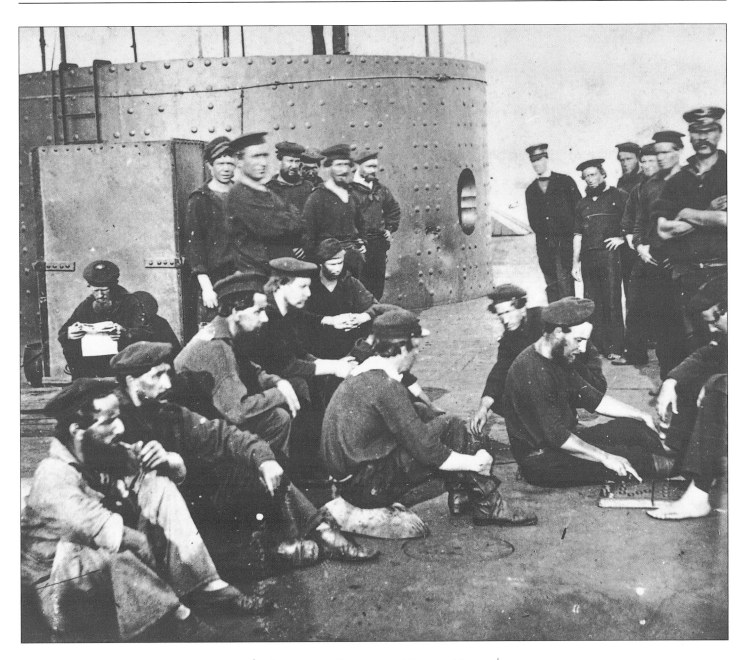

engagement. The Confederate crew was astonished to see that their enemy's guns were aimed at the *Virginia* no matter where she moved. By far the larger of the two vessels, the *Virginia* launched the first volley, firing a ten-gun broadside at the *Monitor*. The turret continued to turn. The *Virginia*'s explosive shells, which easily pierced wooden hulls, did nothing but shake the *Monitor*. The *Virginia* had met her match.

FOUR-HOUR FACE-OFF

The two vessels pounded each other, often at point-blank range. Aboard the *Monitor*, sixteen men were crammed in the turret, eight to a gun. They could not see outside, and received their orders via runner from the pilot house. Inside the turret, the temperature reached 140° F (60° C) degrees. The guns fired 168-pound (76.5kg) solid cannonballs, many of which were deflected upward by the slope of the *Virginia*'s hull, damaging structures above her hull, but not causing serious harm. Likewise, the *Virginia*'s cannons did little more than dent the *Monitor*'s armor. It soon became clear that the *Monitor*'s only vulnerable spots were its gunports.

Like prizefighters, the two ships circled each other for hours. Although the *Monitor*'s shallow draft had been a detriment on the month-long voyage

In July 1862, the crew passed the time on the *Monitor*'s deck while on blockade duty on the James River.

from New York, in the sheltered waters of Hampton Roads the Union ship was far more maneuverable than her counterpart, which was limited to the deeper channels. The *Monitor*'s commander tried to attack the *Virginia*'s unprotected stern, but missed its mark. When the *Monitor* withdrew to secure more ammunition, the *Virginia* headed for the *Minnesota*, but ran aground. With her unarmored lower hull exposed, she was at her most vulnerable. Her crew got her off the bar just as the *Monitor* returned.

Above: A well-known engraving from *Harper's Weekly*, January 24, 1863, shows the ironclad's final desperate moments above the surface. Right: A free-swimming diver illuminates the thick armor belt that shielded the *Monitor* from the *Virginia*'s cannons.

The *Virginia* fired. The exploding shell took out the *Monitor*'s pilot house and blinded her captain. The helmsman moved the ship out of the *Virginia*'s reach.

It was just after noon, and the tide was falling. The *Virginia* had to withdraw to avoid shoaling again.

Both sides claimed victory in what most modern historians consider a standoff. And the world recognized that it had seen the end of the age of oak and canvas battleships.

LOST IN THE GRAVEYARD OF THE ATLANTIC

The *Monitor* and the *Merrimack*, as the *Virginia* remained known through history, never met again. Both sides feared that another engagement might mean the loss of what had proved to be a powerful weapon. Eventually the *Virginia* was scuttled and burned for fear that she would fall into Union hands. The *Monitor*, which spent the rest of her time in Hampton Roads on blockade duty, was relieved in December 1862 by a new ironclad, a vessel of what became known as the Monitor class of ships.

Notorious for her poor navigational abilities on open sea, the *Monitor* was to be towed to Charleston, South Carolina for duty there. The ironclad and the USS *Rhode Island* left Norfolk on December 29. The next day they hit heavy seas as they rounded Cape Hatteras, North Carolina. Stuck below deck, many of the sixty-five men aboard the *Monitor* became seasick as the vessel pitched, but they helped bail as the ship began to leak faster than the steam pumps could dump water overboard.

Around 11 P.M., the *Monitor*'s four-fluked anchor was dropped in the hopes that its more than seven hundred feet (213.4m) of chain would help stabilize the vessel. Instead, the move may have contributed to the ship's sinking. Paying out the anchor chain displaced the packing in the hawsehole, allowing even more water to rush in. By midnight, the incoming sea had doused the boilers, eliminating all power to the ship. With the *Monitor* crippled by a broken towline caught in its port-side paddlewheel, the *Rhode Island* sent its lifeboats to the rescue. Four officers and twelve crewmen were lost, but the rest watched from the *Rhode Island*'s deck as, at about 12:30, the *Monitor*'s red-and-white signal lanterns disappeared.

ANOTHER FIRST FOR THE *MONITOR*

No one set eyes on the ironclad again until 1973. A multi-organizational expedition led by John G. Newton of the Duke University Marine Laboratory found her remains at the edge of the Gulf

Stream about sixteen miles (25.7km) off Cape Hatteras. The *Monitor* lay upside down in some 235 feet (71.7m) of water, her port-stern quarter supported by the revolving gun turret. The following summer, the ship was named to the National Register of Historic Places. Six months later, in January 1975, the wreck site

became the first in a series of national marine sanctuaries administered by the National Oceanic and Atmospheric Administration (NOAA).

The *Monitor* had been identified with remote cameras and closed-circuit television. No one actually visited the wreck until 1977, when scientific divers using surface-supplied mixed gases brought up a red signal lantern and some plating. Two years later, NOAA granted Jacques Cousteau's divers permission to visit the wreck using scuba gear and compressed air, which at such depths acts as a narcotic. By most accounts, the expedition was not productive.

Throughout the 1980s various research organizations visited the Monitor National Marine Sanctuary, all under NOAA's aegis. The Harbor Branch Foundation and Eastern Carolina University raised the ship's unusual

anchor, preserving it and placing it on display at the Mariners' Museum in Newport News, Virginia. The National Trust for Historic Preservation also mounted an expedition. What most of the projects had in common was the use of sophisticated—and expensive—manned and unmanned submersibles, such as the Johnson Sea Link and Deep Drone, the same underwater robot used to recover wreckage from the space shuttle *Challenger*.

A CITIZEN FIGHTS FOR PUBLIC ACCESS

Gary Gentile, a writer, shipwreck researcher, and veteran scuba diver, wasn't content to look at a few artifacts in a museum. He wanted

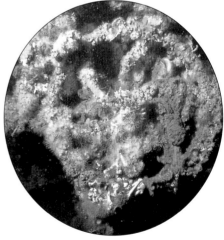

Above: Inside the engine room, a steam gauge (top) and a brass hand wheel are covered with marine growth. Left: With a video camera in a submersible housing mounted atop a diver propulsion vehicle (DPV), or scooter, a diver glides over what remains of the *Monitor*'s gun turret, which now lies askew beneath the ironclad's hull.

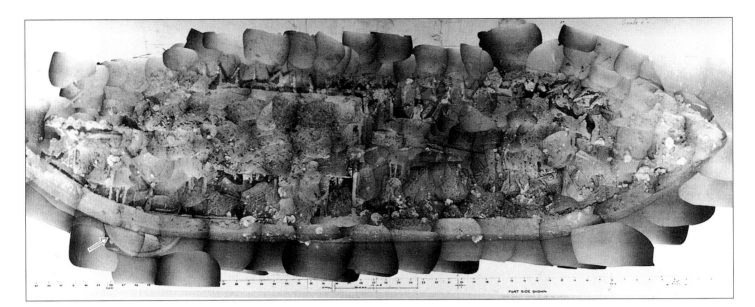

Above: A photomosaic was generated based on 35mm photographs taken remotely by the R/V *Alcoa Seaprobe* during an evaluation cruise conducted by the U.S. Navy in April 1974. Right: Wearing three scuba tanks, a diver examines the *Monitor*'s upside-down stern while a school of amberjack swims overhead.

to see and photograph the *Monitor* himself. He had previously searched for story material at the *Andrea Doria* and other deep East-Coast shipwrecks, and he filed an application with NOAA to dive the *Monitor* in 1984. The agency denied the request on the grounds that the wreck was too deep to be explored safely by free-swimming scuba divers breathing compressed air.

Gentile would not give up. Over the next years he filed eleven applications, some as long as fifty pages with detailed descriptions of dive plans, and got no response from NOAA. In 1986 Gentile's quest caught the attention of Peter Hess, a maritime attorney and avid wreck diver himself. Hess took the case *pro bono*, assuming that it would last only a few months. After all, he reasoned, the federal act that established the marine sanctuaries demanded the widest possible private and public use of those facilities.

Finally, in 1989, Gentile and Hess were granted an administrative hearing. Noting that NOAA had allowed the

Cousteau team to use the same techniques that Gentile proposed—and had, in fact, even expedited the permit—Judge Hugh Dolan granted the divers' request. As for Gentile's safety, Dolan quoted the Idaho Law Review, stating, "A venturesome minority will always be eager to get out on their own, and no obstacles should be placed in their path: let them take risks, for Godsake, let them get lost, sunburnt, stranded, drowned, eaten by bears, buried alive under avalanches—that is the right and privilege of any free American."

In July 1990, Gentile finally set eyes on the *Monitor*.

A DIGITAL RECORD OF DETERIORATION

Ever since the Newton expedition located the *Monitor* in 1973, marine archaeologists have discussed the possibility of raising the wreck. Before proceeding with such a plan, researchers wanted to know the extent and rate of deterioration at the site. Another civilian underwater photographer, Rod Farb, has been working with NOAA to document the *Monitor*'s condition.

Like Gentile, Farb received a permit to dive the *Monitor* using conventional scuba equipment in 1990. Since then he has visited the wreck numerous times, gathering footage with high-resolution video and film cameras. As many as thir-

ty-six thousand images—taken at a specified orientation to the wreck—can be captured in a twenty-minute dive. Later the images are digitized and saved on disk. They can also be printed or converted to slides. Using special software, archaeologists can take detailed measurements from the images at their leisure in the lab, without concern for limited air supply or the need for lengthy decompression procedures.

Although Gentile was denied an opportunity to dive the *Monitor* in 1991 on the grounds that his 1990 photographs were not "scientific," NOAA has since revisited the idea of allowing the general public to visit the wreck without having to perform scientific research at the site. Gentile and Hess have since returned to the sanctuary on several self-funded expeditions, collecting data on deterioration with an ultrasonic instrument that can measure the amount of sound iron versus rust on the wreck.

NOAA also continues to monitor the wreck. In 1993 the agency hired a manned submersible to gather hours of video and to excavate sand around the turret. More than a hundred artifacts have been recovered, preserved, and placed in museums. And a thousand-pound (454kg) permanent anchor has been installed at the site for use by charter boats that will be given permission to bring divers—civilians—to see this piece of American history.

CHAPTER EIGHT

THE RMS RHONE

A SUDDEN STORM STRIKES

The Caribbean sun shone brightly over Peter Island's Great Harbour in the British Virgin Islands. It was the morning of October 29, 1867, and crews loaded cargo and supplies aboard a two-year-old sailing steamship owned and operated by the Royal Mail Steam Packet Company. No one, least of all the passengers, had any inkling that this tenth West Indian cruise would be the last for the RMS *Rhone*. Nor could anyone have imag- ined at the time that more than a hundred years later, the *Rhone* would be one of the world's most frequently visited shipwrecks.

Just over three hundred feet (91.4m) long, the *Rhone* carried passengers and cargo between England and the Caribbean. She had left Southampton on October 2 under the command of Captain Robert F.

Wooley. She was taking on supplies in the British Virgin Islands for the return voyage when the barometer dropped suddenly, the skies blackened, and the sea began to boil. The leading edge of the storm struck from the north-northwest at about 11 A.M., tearing at the ship's rigging with ferocious winds. The *Rhone* took a beating.

The eye of the hurricane passed over about an hour later. Taking advantage of the lull, Captain Wooley ordered the anchor weighed so that the ship could be moved to open water to ride out the rest of the storm. As the crew worked to follow the captain's order, however, a shackle stuck in the vessel's hawsehole, resulting in the loss of the anchor and some three hundred feet (91.4m) of anchor chain. The *Rhone*'s powerful engines were set at full speed, and Wooley set a course for open sea through the rocky waters of Sir Francis Drake Channel. In the meantime, the eye had passed, and the storm struck with renewed force from the south-southeast. As the *Rhone* neared Salt Island she was dashed against the rocks. She broke in two and sank instantly to the bottom.

Only a few survived the disaster. One crewman clung to the forward topsail for seventeen hours until he was rescued. The hurricane sank or seriously damaged seventy-five vessels, including the *Rhone*, and destroyed all but eighteen houses on the nearby island of Tortola. Some five hundred lives were lost in the late-season storm.

THE *RHONE* BECOMES A REEF

The *Rhone* came to rest in about ninety feet (27.4m) of water off Black Rock Point at the southwest tip of Salt Island,

Left: Built in England in 1865, the *Rhone* has rested on the floor of the Carribean for 130 years. Top, Right: Encrusted with corals and sponges, the wreck has become home to large schools of colorful Caribbean reef fish. Right: The *Rhone*'s cannon lies pinned beneath the wreckage at the end of the bow section.

with some parts of her wreckage rising to within fifteen to twenty feet (4.6 to 6.1m) of the surface. Not long after her sinking, divers salvaged much of her cargo, including bales of cotton and bottles of brandy and champagne. As time passed, the *Rhone*'s remains became encrusted with corals and colorful sponges, and her hull was home to a rainbow of reef fish: yellow-tail snappers, sergeant majors, Spanish hogfish, blackbar soldierfish, and other species. In 1980 the government of the British Virgin Islands declared the wreck site the RMS *Rhone* National Park. Fishing of any kind, removal of artifacts or marine life, and anchoring are all prohibited in the protected area. A series of mooring buoys has been installed to accommodate the sailing yachts and charter boats that bring hundreds of scuba divers and snorkelers to visit the site daily.

The *Rhone*'s anchor, discovered in the harbor at Peter Island by a local diver in 1974, is also protected under the national park system.

Left: Made of iron, these arches in the *Rhone*'s midsection have withstood 130 years of saltwater submersion. Nearby are a winch, a set of enormous wrenches, and the broken remains of one of the ship's boilers. Above: A marker reminds visiting divers that the *Rhone* site is a National Marine Park where removing artifacts or disturbing marine life is forbidden.

A MOVIE SET
AND A SIGHT TO SEE

The *Rhone*'s wreckage covers an area of about sixteen hundred square feet (488 sq. m). The bow section, approximately one hundred and fifty feet (45.8m) long, lies on its starboard side. Divers who cruise along this nearly intact portion of hull will easily recognize the ship's bowsprit. Swimming aft, they'll encounter an intact porthole and a hatchway that was used during the filming of some of the underwater scenes in the movie *The Deep*. Continuing on, divers will see the foremast; those who follow it out into the sand can find the remains of the crow's nest. One of the *Rhone*'s two cannons lies in the sand just forward of where the ship broke in half. Nearby are the davits from the lifeboats that were never launched.

In slightly shallower water, the stern is often visited by snorkelers or by divers on a second dive. The deepest features in this section, at roughly sixty feet (18.3m), are the *Rhone*'s water pump and one of its two boilers. An eighty-foot-long (24.4m) portion of the propeller shaft points toward shore from the ship's gearbox. The broken stern mast lies parallel to it out in the sand. On the port side a row of brass portholes still gleams. At the wreck's shallowest point, in fifteen to thirty feet (4.6 to 9.1m) of water, are the rudder and two blades of the ship's bronze propeller which, though powerful, could not outrun the storm.

Above: A Spanish hogfish swims through a porthole on the RMS *Rhone*, a nineteenth-century sailing steamship that is now a prime attraction for divers visiting the British Virgin Islands.
Right: Many of the fish that inhabit the wreckage of the sunken *Rhone* are quite accustomed to divers and snorkelers who visit the site by the hundreds each day. Some may even be so brazen as to follow a diver, hoping for hand-outs, but most seem content to go about their business seemingly oblivious to the human intrusion.

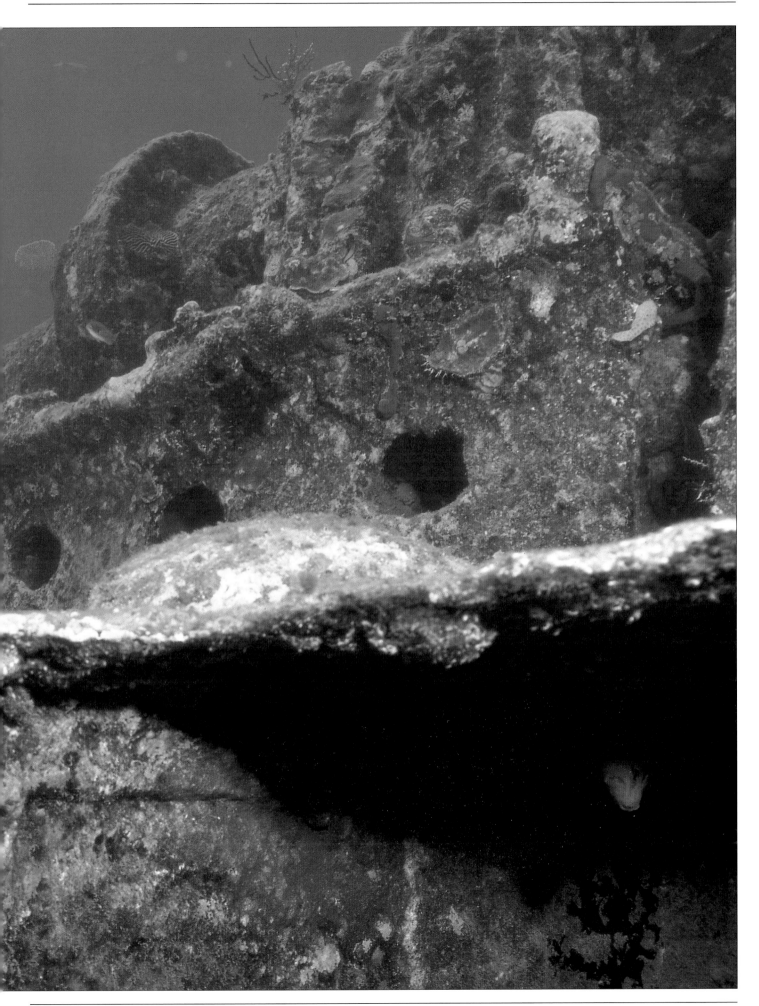

CHAPTER NINE

THE WHITE STAR LINER RMS *TITANIC*

THE SHIP OF DREAMS MEETS DISASTER

The sleek liner slicing through the North Atlantic night was said to be unsinkable—but she was fated never to complete her maiden voyage. By morning her mortal hull would come to rest more than two miles (3.2km) below the surface of the sea, taking with her some fifteen hundred souls. Ironically, the tragedy itself may have earned the ship its immortality, for she remains alive to this day in the hearts and imaginations of people around the world. It can safely be said that no shipwreck is better known than the *Titanic*.

WHITE STAR'S SHINING JEWEL

On the night of April 14, 1912, the moonless sky was clear and full of stars, and barely a breath of air disturbed the mirror-like surface of the waters as the Royal Mail Ship *Titanic* steamed across the Atlantic. Built for the White Star Line, the new ship boasted a double hull with sixteen watertight compartments. At just over 882 feet (268.8m) long, she had eleven decks and could carry more than thirty-five hundred passengers and crew at a top speed of nearly twenty-five knots. Among the *Titanic's* amenities were four restaurants, a theater,

Left: Built by Harland & Wolff, the *Titanic* was the largest ship afloat when she made her first and final journey in April 1912. Right: While the *Titanic* radio operators wired frantically for help from this room, the radio operator of the nearest ship, the *Californian*, had gone to bed. The same ship had tried to warn the *Titanic* of icebergs earlier that night.

a Turkish bath, facilities for miniature golf, tennis and squash, and a pet kennel.

When the *Titanic* picked up the last of her passengers from Queenstown, Ireland on April 11, she had more than twenty-two hundred people aboard. (Actual totals vary from 2,208 to 2,227, due to discrepancies on the passenger and crew lists.) Among the passengers to New York were eleven millionaires, including Colonel John Jacob Astor and his pregnant bride Madeleine; mining magnate Benjamin Guggenheim; Harry Molson of the banking and brewing family; and Isidor Straus, who owned Macy's, and his wife, Ida. J. Bruce Ismay, president of the White Star line, was also aboard. The ship was under the command of Captain Edward J. Smith, who planned to retire at the end of the cruise.

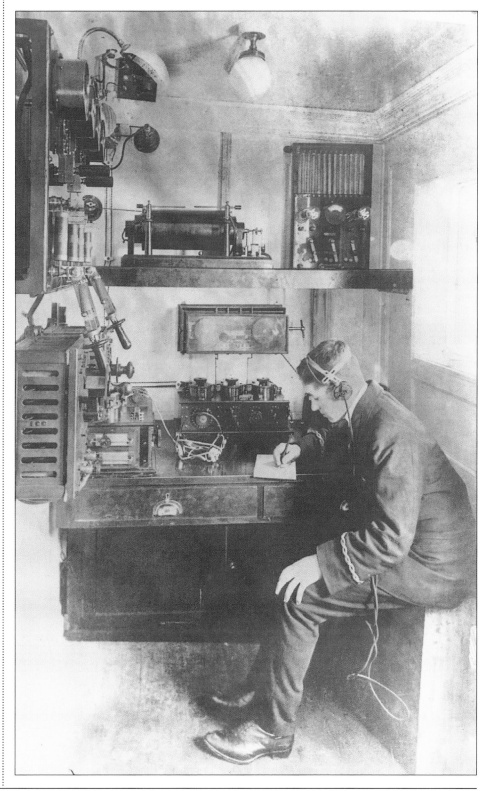

Top: The iceberg that sank the *Titanic* was about as tall as the boat deck above water, the highest deck on the ship. Above: Marconi operator Jack Phillips was busy sending passengers' personal messages when the final ice warning came in shortly before the collision.

ICEBERGS AND IRONIES

By 11:40 P.M. the liner was approximately four hundred miles (643.6km) southeast of Newfoundland. Although ice was more common farther north, it was not unknown along the *Titanic*'s course. In fact, the ship's wireless radio operators had received at least seven warnings from other ships; the last came at 11 P.M. from the *Californian*. Wireless technology was relatively new, and not all ships carried radios. Although the *Titanic* was well equipped, its radio operators worked for a private company and no protocol had been established for carrying messages from the Marconi room to the officers on the ship's bridge. When the *Californian*'s message came in the *Titanic*'s operator had just established a clear connection with the wireless station at Newfoundland's Cape Race and was busy sending personal messages from passengers.

The ship was cruising at a speed of at least twenty-two knots when the lookouts in the crow's nest spotted an iceberg dead ahead and alerted the bridge.

The engines were stopped, and the helmsman steered the ship to port, trying to veer away from the deadly obstacle off the bow—but too late. The *Titanic* was too large, and moving too quickly, to respond.

Most passengers felt only a slight jolt or heard a scraping sound as the *Titanic* hit the iceberg along the starboard bow. Many were unaware of the collision until the ship began to list as six of her compartments filled with water. Captain Smith surveyed the damage below decks and saw that the liner was doomed. Not long after midnight, he gave the order to abandon ship.

TERROR AND A TOUCH OF CLASS

With the deck tilting toward the sea, women and children were ushered into the lifeboats. In the panic and confusion, the first few boats were launched before they were full, and the terrible truth soon became clear: the *Titanic's* twenty lifeboats could only accommodate about one-third of the people aboard. Unless a rescue ship arrived, the rest would drown or freeze to death in the icy waters.

Understandably, many passengers were stricken with terror. Yet others demonstrated a level of composure that would become part of the *Titanic* legend. Ida Straus chose to stay with the sinking ship rather than board a lifeboat and leave her husband behind. Benjamin Guggenheim donned formal evening clothes so that he could "die like a gen-

Survivors in lifeboats frantically rowed away from the sinking ship to avoid being capsized as the inevitable came to pass.

The lucky passengers who made it into lifeboats waited hours in the frigid night to be rescued. Eventually they were taken aboard the *Carpathia*, which was sixty miles (96km) away when she received the *Titanic*'s distress call at 12:15 A.M.

lifeboats heard the agonized cries of the victims thrown into the 28° F (-2° C) degree water, until they gradually faded into the night. Two hours later the *Carpathia* picked up the first of the survivors, ultimately rescuing about seven hundred people.

TITANIC IMPACT: THE SINKING CHANGED EVERYTHING

Ten days after the tragedy, the crew of the *Titanic*'s twin-sister ship *Olympic* went on strike because the vessel did not have enough lifeboats. In the following weeks an inquiry found the White Star Line guilty of negligence for its lack of lifeboats and inadequate lifeboat drills, and ordered more watertight compartments for ships. The following year the International Convention for Safety of Life at Sea was established. The Convention instituted lifeboat regulations and required that wireless radios be operated and manned around the clock. The formation of the International Ice Patrol was also a result of the *Titanic* catastrophe.

The calamity caught the world's imagination and continues to reverberate in history. The loss of the "unsinkable" liner marked the end of an era of unquestioning confidence in human technology. Newspapers of the time used the sinking as an opportunity to comment on topics ranging from hubris and heroism to women's suffrage. The *Titanic*'s story has spawned dozens of books and a number of films, many of which treat the sinking as a morality play. Others examine why this shipwreck, more than any other, has been given such significance by so many. The *Empress of Ireland*, which sank in the St. Lawrence River in 1914 with a similar loss of life, never developed such a fervent following. Nor does interest in the

tleman." The band played the Episcopal hymn "Autumn."

Less than twenty miles (32.1km) away, the wireless operator on the *Californian* had shut down his station and gone to bed, never hearing the *Titanic*'s calls for help. The SS *Carpathia* responded

to the message, but would take hours to reach the sinking ship's reported location.

From the *Titanic* came a final radio call, "Sinking by the head." At 2:20 A.M. the bow sank. A moment later the stern righted itself, then stood on end and plunged into the abyss. Those in the

Titanic seem to be waning. Even today, the *Titanic* provides subject matter for historical societies, documentaries, movies, television miniseries, sites on the World Wide Web, and even computer games and a Broadway musical!

DISCOVERY OF THE CENTURY

Interest in the *Titanic* has never been limited to the event and its meaning. Ever since the sinking, groups of people have wanted to probe the wreck itself. Initially, relatives of some of the victims chartered a boat to drop dynamite in the vicinity, in the hope that the remains of their loved ones would surface. The venture was unsuccessful. Later efforts focused on locating and raising the ship. The Disney organization spent tens of thousands of dollars on a feasibility study, but later dropped the project. In the 1980s Texas millionaire Jack Grimm financed three expeditions to locate the wreckage.

TITANIC FOUND BY FRANCO-AMERICAN TEAM

In the summer of 1985, the French ship *Le Suroit* spent a month surveying the bottom of the Atlantic off Newfoundland. They used a submarine sonar unit specially designed for the two-and-a-half-mile (4km) depths in the search area. The ship was part of a joint expedition by the Deep Submergence Laboratory of the Woods Hole Oceanographic Institute, the French Institute for Research and Exploitation of the Sea (IFREMER), and the National Geographic Society, under the direction of Dr. Robert D. Ballard and Jean-Louis Michel. The United States Navy funded the expedition, which provided an opportunity to test *Argo*, a four-thousand-pound (1,816kg), sled-mounted deep-water television camera system engineered to operate at extreme depths.

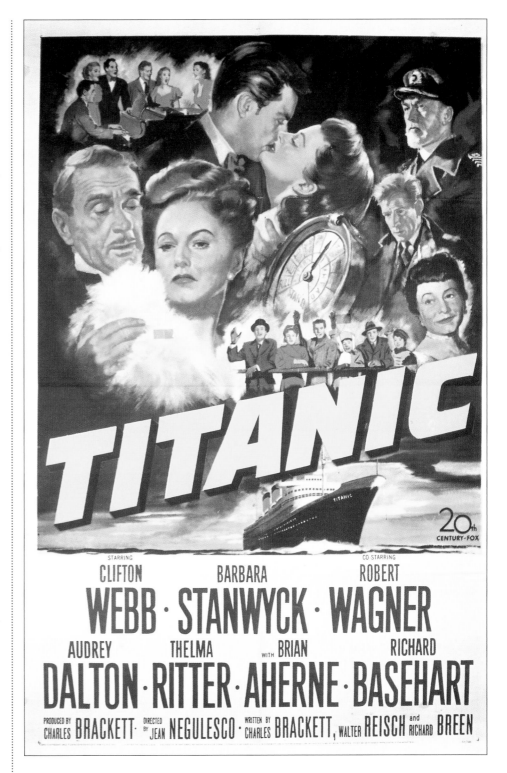

With all the elements of a morality play, the *Titanic* tragedy has inspired eight feature films, dozens of books—both nonfiction accounts and novelizations—a TV miniseries, and a Broadway musical.

In August the French ship was relieved by the R/V (research vessel) *Knorr*, equipped with the remotely operated *ANGUS* (Acoustically Navigated Geological Underwater Survey) deep-sea still camera system and *Argo*. Like the sonar, the cameras had to be able to withstand more than six thousand pounds (2,724kg) of pressure per square inch (2.5 sq. cm). Using *Argo*, the team investigated sonar targets from *Le Suroit* and previous expeditions. Those possibilities exhausted, the search was moved eastward.

On September 1, 1985, just before 1 A.M., the cry of "Wreckage!" was heard from *Argo*'s control center on *Knorr*'s back deck. A ship's boiler surrounded by debris appeared on the video screen.

The *Titanic*'s hull lay in two sections in 12,460 feet (3,797.8m) of water surrounded by undersea sand dunes. From the debris field in between, *Argo*'s powerfully lit cameras retrieved pictures of luggage, wine cases, and other items that spilled from the broken ship when it sank to the bottom. The expedition returned with poignant images, including a photograph of an empty lifeboat davit on the starboard bow, but the scientists wanted to know more. And Ballard wanted to see the wreck for himself.

The following summer Ballard returned to the *Titanic* for twelve days aboard the *Atlantis II*. The *Atlantis* carried the *Alvin* three-person submersible, built of titanium to explore depths to thirteen thousand feet (3,962.4m), and *Jason Junior*, a remote-controlled underwater robot known affectionately as "the swimming eyeball." These tools allowed much greater access to the wreck than *Argo* and ANGUS. With *Jason Junior* linked to the sub via a 250-foot (76.2m) tether, Ballard was able to sit inside *Alvin* on the *Titanic*'s deck and send the robot and its cameras inside the wreck. Among the areas photographed was the once-opulent Grand Staircase. Chandeliers covered with marine growth still hung from the first-class foyer where millionaires once walked.

The New York Times.

TITANIC SINKS FOUR HOURS AFTER HITTING ICEBERG; 866 RESCUED BY CARPATHIA, PROBABLY 1250 PERISH; ISMAY SAFE, MRS. ASTOR MAYBE, NOTED NAMES MISSING

CAPT. E. J. SMITH, Commander of the Titanic.

The Lost Titanic Being Towed Out of Belfast Harbor.

SPLIT AT THE SEAMS

Along with *Jason Junior*'s cameras, the view through *Alvin*'s portholes enabled Ballard to assess the wreck's condition. Her bow, upright but mired in sixty feet (18.3m) of mud, was no candidate for salvage. With the exception of some teak, most of the wood had been eaten away. Reddish-orange "rustcicles" covered most of the metal, crumbling and destroying visibility when touched.

Below: Aboard the *Carpathia*, survivors crowded the rail to get a welcome glimpse of land as the Cunard liner neared Sandy Hook, New Jersey, on its approach to New York Harbor. Right: On the cutter *Modoc*, members of the International Ice Patrol held a memorial service for those lost in the sinking.

Ballard found no evidence of the three-hundred-foot (91.4m) gash that the iceberg was said to have caused. But much of the starboard side is buried up to the anchor, still in its hawsehole. Instead, it appeared as though some of the ship's hull plates had buckled on impact, coming loose at the seams. In March 1995 a five-person team of American naval architects and marine engineers studied available reports. They determined that the *Titanic*'s sinking was due to a combination of poor building materials, including faulty rivets, and a rudder that was too small to turn a ship of the *Titanic*'s size traveling at the swift liner's speed. Other researchers continue to seek a definitive answer. Sophisticated sonar capable of penetrating the mud surrounding the bow may hold the key.

EXPEDITION RAISES ARTIFACTS—AND A FUROR

In 1987, a group of investors organized by George Tulloch, a former car salesman from Connecticut, hired IFREMER's submarine *Nautile* and the robot *Robin* to explore the wreck. Beginning in July the group spent nearly two months at the site, taking hundreds of photographs. They also recovered artifacts, including plates, bottles, and one of the ship's safes. The opening of the safe on live television was the highlight of a documentary aired following the expedition.

The salvage operation became the center of controversy. Many people—including Ballard and members of the Titanic Historical Society—criticized the expedition. Some decried it as grave-robbing, although no human remains had

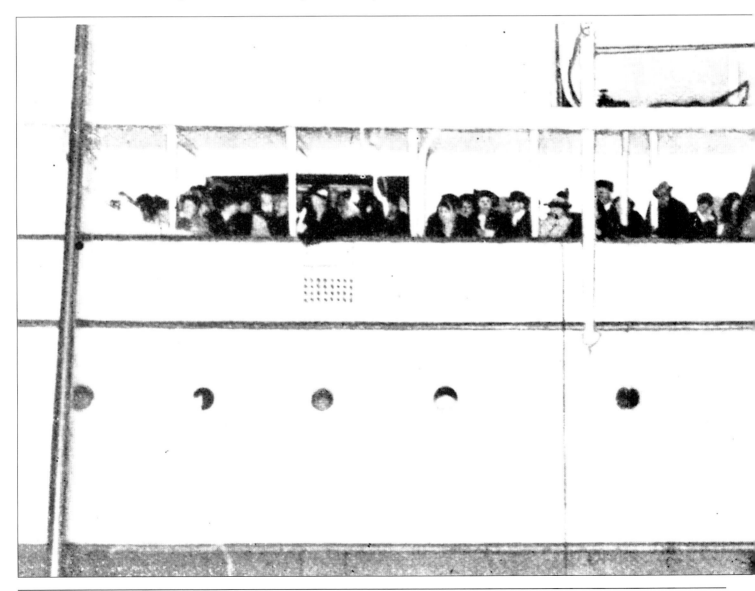

ever been found at the site. Others felt that items should be recovered and displayed for the world to see. Still others were not opposed to the artifact recovery itself as much as the idea that it was being done for commercial gain. Few were without an opinion, and various *Titanic* societies around the world still protest that the wreck should remain undisturbed. The U.S. Congress passed a resolution to make the wreck, which lies in international waters, a memorial, but Great Britain and France were not receptive to the idea. Tulloch's group gets to decide what will happen to the recovered items, but he has said that he will not sell them.

BRINGING BACK THE PAST

Thousands of items from the *Titanic* have since been salvaged, preserved, and put on display. At least one of them found a particularly fitting home. *Titanic* survivor Edith Haisman was presented with the watch that her father was wearing when he watched his sixteen-year-old daughter and her mother climb aboard a lifeboat the night of the sinking. Eventually the family will donate the piece to a museum in Southampton, England, whence the *Titanic* embarked on its first and only journey.

RMS *Titanic*, Inc., with George Tulloch at its helm, returned to the wreck in 1996. Their ambitious plan was to gather documentary footage, study the wreck site further, and raise a section of the hull to the surface. Crew members included a microbial biologist to study bacteria on the wreck and try to determine the rate of the hull's deterioration. Also aboard the research ship *Nadir* were two naval architects, one of whom was a representative from Harland and Wolff, the Belfast shipyard that built the *Titanic*. The submarine *Nautile* was supported by a range of technology including two mini-submersibles and a computerized system that linked sonar information with Global Positioning System data for navigation and tracking.

The expedition was more than high-tech—it was *wired*. An on-board correspondent uploaded daily progress reports to The Discovery Channel's site on the World Wide Web via satellite telephone. Another topside ship, the *Ocean Voyager*, had a complete television production facility. And at the end of August two passenger ships brought thousands of *Titanic* buffs to the site to witness the raising of a twenty-one-ton (19,068kg) hull segment.

THE *TITANIC* SINKS A SECOND TIME

The salvors planned to use ten lift bags filled with five thousand pounds (2,270kg) of diesel fuel, which is lighter than water, to raise a chunk of hull twenty-four feet (7.3m) long by sixteen feet (4.9m) high. Only six of the bags were attached successfully. The ballast system of two of the attached bags failed to release. The four remaining bags, however, provided enough buoyancy to lift the metal, suspended by nylon cords, to within about two hundred feet (61m) of the surface.

For nine hours the crew worked in rough seas to rig the piece securely so that it could be winched aboard the salvage ship *Kilabuk*. Despite their efforts the winch could not raise the hull segment any higher. As the waves grew higher, the team decided to try to tow the segment to the shallower waters of the Grand Banks where the mini-submersibles could inspect the rigging. Before the ship could get underway, the four nylon tethers broke one by one and the hull of the unsinkable *Titanic* drifted back to the bottom.

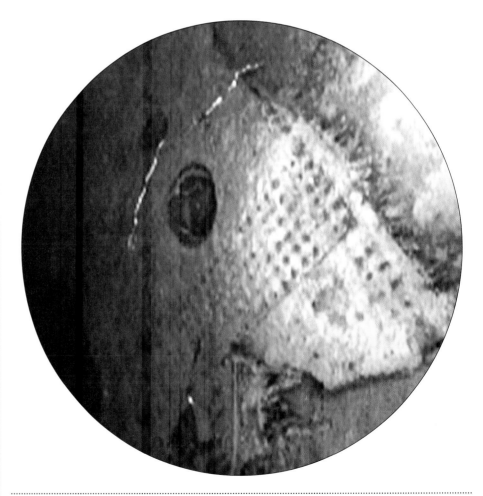

Above: A section of the *Titanic*'s steel hull lies on the floor of the Atlantic Ocean off Newfoundland, where it fell during an unsuccessful salvage attempt in the summer of 1996. Right: Miles below the surface, the *Titanic*'s bow sits silently, covered with rust, daring explorers to unravel its mysteries.

CHAPTER TEN

THE LUSITANIA

THE FIGHTING CONTINUES OVER WORLD WAR I TORPEDO VICTIM

I f the passengers climbing the gangway to board the *Lusitania* on May 1, 1915, had seen that day's edition of *The New York Sun*, they might have made other travel plans.

For eight years the liner had cruised between New York City and Liverpool, England. On May 1, the day the ship was to leave New York, a notice appeared in the *Sun*, near the *Lusitania*'s departure schedule. The warning also appeared in nearly fifty other newspapers around the United States. It read:

NOTICE! TRAVELERS intending to embark on the Atlantic voyage are reminded that a state of war exists between Germany and her allies, and Great Britain and her allies; that the zone of war includes the waters adjacent to the British Isles; that in accordance with formal notice given by the Imperial German Government, vessels

Top: The *Lusitania* and her sister ship, *Mauretania*, were among the fastest vessels serving the New York–to–Liverpool route. Right: The second-class smoking room was opulently decorated in Edwardian elegance, from its elaborately decorated domed ceiling to its luxurious patterned carpet.

flying the flag of Great Britain, or any of her allies, are liable to destruction in those waters and that travelers sailing in the war zone on ships of Great Britain or her allies do so at their own risk.

IMPERIAL GERMAN EMBASSY
Washington, D.C., April 22, 1915

Although the advertisement had been sent in April, some sources say that the U.S. State Department—intentionally or otherwise—withheld approval to print the warning until May 1. Telegrams warning passengers about the message were held at the Cunard office for later delivery. A few people canceled their passages, but most chose to sail. No one thought that the German Navy had the audacity to target a ship with so many Americans aboard when the United States was not involved in the conflict. Besides, they reasoned, with a top speed of twenty-five knots, the *Lusitania* could outrun any German U-boat.

ONE TORPEDO, TWO EXPLOSIONS, AND MANY QUESTIONS

The Atlantic crossing took about a week and was uneventful. Captain William Turner was confident. Although one of the *Lusitania's* boilers was out of commission, preventing the liner from reaching top speed, she could still run if she had to. Turner also was expecting the cruiser *Juno* to escort his vessel into Liverpool. He was unaware that on May 5, due to U-boat sightings off the Irish coast, all British ships, including the *Juno*, had been ordered out of the area.

The *Lusitania* was running at about eighteen knots as she approached the Old Head of Kinsale, a lighthouse on Ireland's southeast coast, on May 7. Contrary to orders, Turner ran a straight course

Through the periscope, the crew of the U-20 submarine spotted "four funnels, schooner rig, upwards of 25,000 tons (22,700,000kg), speed about 22 knots," then fired at their target.

instead of zigzagging to elude enemy submarines. And as he neared land, he slowed down to take a navigational heading. About twelve miles (19.3km) from shore, silhouetted by the headlands, the liner was a perfect target.

The *U-20*, a German submarine under the command of Lieutenant Karl Schweiger, sighted the *Lusitania*. At 1:40 P.M. the U-boat fired a single torpedo, striking the liner's starboard side just aft of the first funnel. The projectile exploded on impact. A moment later a second blast, the cause of which is unknown, rocked the ship. The liner began to sink immediately, her deck so steeply canted that many of the lifeboats could not be launched. She sank in less than twenty minutes, taking twelve hundred of her

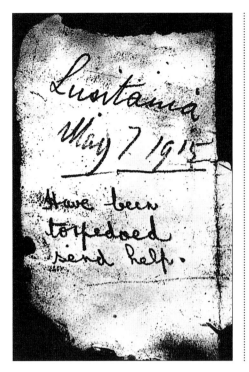

1,959 passengers to the bottom. Among the victims were 128 Americans and thirty-five infants-in-arms. Fewer than five hundred bodies were ever recovered.

MYTHS AND MYSTERIES

Americans were outraged. Even before the sinking, Secretary of State William Jennings Bryan had wanted to restrict

Left: This note was found in a bottle buried on an English beach. Its origin has never been traced. Below: Passengers and crew of the *Lusitania* tried to hang onto lifeboats and rafts when the ship went down, but many perished before help arrived.

Americans from traveling in the submarine zones. President Woodrow Wilson disagreed and held his ground following the tragedy. Bryan resigned. Yet, contrary to popular belief, the United States maintained its official position of neutrality for two years after the *Lusitania*'s sinking. President Wilson did not ask Congress to declare war on Germany until April 1917, after the sinking of the U.S. supply ship *Illinois*.

Although there is no record that Lieutenant Schweiger had specific orders to hunt the *Lusitania*, historians have reason to believe that the vessel was not a random target. Germany claimed that the ship was secretly carrying munitions for Great Britain and was therefore a legitimate "kill." Although the German claim

"All the News That's Fit to Print."

The New York Times.

EXTRA 5:30 A. M.

VOL. LXIV...NO. 20,923. NEW YORK, SATURDAY, MAY 8, 1915.—TWENTY-FOUR PAGES. ONE CENT

LUSITANIA SUNK BY A SUBMARINE, PROBABLY 1,260 DEAD; TWICE TORPEDOED OFF IRISH COAST; SINKS IN 15 MINUTES; CAPT. TURNER SAVED, FROHMAN AND VANDERBILT MISSING; WASHINGTON BELIEVES THAT A GRAVE CRISIS IS AT HAND

SHOCKS THE PRESIDENT

Washington Deeply Stirred by the Loss of American Lives.

BULLETINS AT WHITE HOUSE

Wilson Reads Them Closely, but Is Silent on the Nation's Course.

HINTS OF CONGRESS CALL

Loss of Lusitania Recalls Firm Tone of Our First Warning to Germany.

CAPITAL FULL OF RUMORS

Reports That Liner Was to be Sunk Were Heard Before Actual News Came.

Special to The New York Times.

WASHINGTON, May 7.—Never since that April day, three years ago, when word came that the Titanic had gone down, has Washington been so stirred as it is tonight over the sinking of the Lusitania. The early reports told that there had been no loss of life, but the relief that these advices caused gave way to the greatest concern late this evening when it became known that there had been many deaths. Although they are profoundly reticent, officials realize that this tragedy, involving the loss of American citizens, is likely to bring about a crisis in the international relations of the United States.

It is pointed out that the sinking of the Lusitania is the outcome of a series of incidents that have been the cause of concern to this Government in its endeavor to maintain a strictly neutral position in the great European war.

Nation's Course in Doubt.

It is impossible to say tonight what effect the loss of American lives on the Lusitania will have on the Government. Judged from the little that can be learned it is a safe prediction that President Wilson will endeavor

The Lost Cunard Steamship Lusitania

SOME DEAD TAKEN ASHORE

Several Hundred Survivors at Queenstown and Kinsale.

STEWARD TELLS OF DISASTER

...do Crashes Into the

Cunard Office Here Besieged for News; Fate of 1,918 on Lusitania Long in Doubt

Nothing Heard from the Well-Known Passengers on Board—Story of Disaster Long Unconfirmed While Anxious Crowds Seek Details.

Official news of the sinking of the Lusitania yesterday reached New York in fragmentary reports, and several hours elapsed between the first unverified rumor of the disaster and the cable messages that told at night of the saving of some of the passengers and gave meagre details of the most sensational incident of its kind in the war.

The early accounts that indicated all on board had been saved reassured hundreds of friends and relatives of pas-

List of Saved Includes Capt. Turner; Vanderbilt and Frohman Reported Lost

LONDON, Saturday, May 8, 5:30 A. M.—The Press Bureau has received from the British Admiralty at Queenstown a report that all the torpedo boats and tugs and armed trawlers, except the Heron, which went out from Queenstown to the relief of the Lusitania have returned.

These vessels have landed 595 survivors and forty dead. Fifty-two more survivors are reported aboard a steamer, while eleven others and five bodies have been landed at Kinsale, making the total number of survivors 658, besides forty-five dead. The numbers will be verified later, and it is considered possible Kinsale fishing boats may have rescued a few more.

Among the survivors is the Captain of the Lusitania, William T. Turner. Some of the survivors at Queenstown say that Alfred Gwynne Vanderbilt was drowned. Every effort to find Mr. Vanderbilt and Charles Frohman, the theatrical manager, among the survivors has failed.

Saw the Submarine 100 Y... and Watched Torpedo as...

Ernest Cowper, a Toronto Newspa... Attack, Seen from Ship's Rai... Used in Torpedoes, Say Othe...

Queenstown, Saturday, May 8, 3:18 A. M.

A sharp lookout for submarines was kept aboard the Lusitania as she approached the Irish coast, according to Ernest Cowper, a Toronto newspaper man, who was among the survivors landed at

ADVERTISEMENT.

NOTICE!

TRAVELLERS intending to embark on the Atlantic voyage are reminded that a state of war exists between Germany and her allies and Great Britain and her allies; that the zone of war includes the waters adjacent to the British Isles; that, in accordance with formal notice given by the Imperial German Government, vessels flying the flag of Great Britain, or of any of her allies, are liable to destruction in those waters and that travellers sailing in the war zone on ships of Great Britain or her allies do so at their own risk.

IMPERIAL GERMAN EMBASSY

WASHINGTON, D. C., APRIL 22, 1915.

LONDON, Saturday, May ...—The Cunard liner Lusitania, which sailed out of New York last Saturday with 1,918 souls

Though the sinking caused a tremendous furor, as seen on this cover of the *New York Times*, it was still not enough to draw the United States into the war between Germany and Great Britain.

has never been proven, shipping records indicate that the passenger steamer may have been carrying more than twelve hundred cases of three-inch (7.6cm) cannon shells along with tons of gun cotton, which becomes highly unstable when it reacts with water. This could explain the second explosion. Alternatively, the second explosion could simply have been due to coal dust build-up from the boilers.

Stories and unsubstantiated rumors about the *Lusitania* abound. Some believe that the ship was intentionally sacrificed by Great Britain in hopes of dragging the United States into the Great War. Another popular tale concerns the possibility that the liner went down with $272 million in gold bullion.

One intriguing story, apparently true, has yet to be resolved. One of the sinking victims was Sir Hugh Lane, a director of the National Gallery of Ireland, who was returning home after a purchasing trip to New York. He is believed to have been transporting more than two dozen priceless paintings by Rubens, Monet, and other masters. Lane was last seen helping women and children into lifeboats. If the artwork he carried was sealed in lead or zinc cylinders, as some think it was, it might have been preserved from the ravages of the sea.

DISPUTED OWNERSHIP

Lying in three hundred feet (91.4m) of water, the *Lusitania* was left alone for the better part of fifty years. In the last thirty years, however, the vessel's remains have been the subject

of underwater research, salvage attempts, and courtroom controversy.

In the 1960s John Light, a former U.S. Navy diver, purchased the rights to salvage the *Lusitania*'s hull and machinery for one thousand pounds sterling from the British War Risks Insurance Association. Using Aqua-Lungs (early diving equipment), Light and his team explored the wreck over a period of years, trying to determine whether it had in fact carried munitions. Light passed away in 1992, and the results of his research have never been published.

In 1982 a commercial salvage operation, backed by New Mexico venture

Left: The luxurious liner featured handsomely carved moldings and the finest furnishings of mahogany and leather. Pictured here is the Grand Salon. Below: The diamond pattern visible on the *Lusitania*'s carpet can still be seen today, although it is becoming covered with sea anemones.

capitalist and plumbing fixtures heir F. Gregg Bemis Jr., brought up three of the ship's manganese bronze propellers, along with dishes and silverware. Bemis, who claims to have purchased salvage rights from one of Light's former partners, had one of the propellers melted and cast into thirty-five hundred sets of golf clubs. The sets sold for nine thousand dollars each.

Bemis hired saturation divers from Oceaneering International to do the salvage job. Saturation divers spend hours working underwater, then hours more decompressing in a special pressurized chamber designed to prevent them from getting the bends as excessive nitrogen leaves their tissues. A decade later *Titanic* discoverer Dr. Robert Ballard and the National Geographic Society used small manned submarines and submersible robots to explore the areas around the ship's magazine and the spot where the torpedo struck. By overlaying Computer-Assisted Design drawings on digitized images of the broken wreckage, the explorers were able to determine exactly where on the ship they were searching. The robot enabled them to explore beneath overhangs and other areas where the subs would not fit and where a diver might have been in jeopardy.

BACK TO (MORE OR LESS) BASICS

In 1994, two years after Ballard's expedition, divers once again visited the *Lusitania* using only the equipment that they carried with them. Even so, technology had changed significantly since the time Light and his team worked the site breathing compressed air. An Anglo-American group of twelve scuba enthusiasts organized by British filmmaker Polly Tapson used a breathing gas called trimix, which included helium to offset the narcotic properties of standard air. They had trained for years to make the dives, which by recreational scuba training standards were dangerously deep. Tapson and her fellow divers made a total of about a hundred dives on the

A 1996 Irish High Court decision gave an American millionaire ownership of the *Lusitania*'s hull and fittings, such as this porthole. Currently, Ireland retains rights to the vessel's cargo.

Lusitania over the course of two weeks. Tapson told the press that the team saw cylinders in the sand, which might have been the type used to transport the lost paintings. American author and photographer Gary Gentile, who had earlier fought to open the USS *Monitor* to access by sport divers, captured the wreck on film.

What might have been an adventuresome dive holiday turned into a legal case. Not convinced by Bemis's claims of ownership, Tapson's group dived the wreck over the millionaire's protests. Following their dives, Bemis tried to sue for criminal trespass. He also insisted that he owned the rights to all photographs taken of the wreck and any other intellectual property that resulted from the dives.

IRELAND ENTERS THE FRAY

Bemis wasn't the only one who was making claims on the wreck. John Light's widow Muriel also claimed an interest, which was later settled out of court. The four Americans who participated in Tapson's expedition formed Fifty Fathom Ventures to stake a claim of their own—which was quickly dismissed. Then the Irish Ministry of Arts and Culture imposed a Maritime Heritage Order on the wreck, which lies in Irish waters. The order prohibits anyone from diving on the ship without the agency's permission. Most recently, courts in the United States and Ireland have ruled that Bemis does, indeed, own the rights to the *Lusitania*'s hull and fittings. Tapson's group was never prosecuted for criminal trespass; they have published material based on expedition, but state that the moneys from publishing have been donated to diving research. Bemis continues to fight Ireland's claims to the cargo and personal effects aboard the sunken liner. And if priceless paintings are found undamaged in sealed cylinders, the battle promises to be a long one.

CHAPTER ELEVEN

THE SHIPWRECKS OF SCAPA FLOW

SINKINGS IN A STRATEGIC HARBOR

Negotiations at Versailles were at a stalemate. Germany balked at the humiliating terms of surrender; Great Britain threatened military action. As the world waited to see if The Great War (now known as World War I) was truly at an end, the commander of Kaiser Wilhelm's German High Seas Fleet arranged to scuttle seventy-four of his own ships, which were interned in the Scottish harbor known as Scapa Flow. Admiral Ludwig von Reuter would rather

As pictured below and to the right, seventy-four German warships were scuttled in the Scottish harbor of Scapa Flow, sinking almost defiantly before the eyes of their enemies—and later creating a cottage salvage industry in the Orkney Islands.

The rusting remains of the 8,900 gross ton (8,081,200kg) *Inverlane* lie only partially submerged in the waters of Orkney's Burra Sound. The tanker was the largest of several "blockships" sunk intentionally to barricade Scapa Flow.

sink his beloved fleet than see the British claim the vessels as spoils of war.

Separated from the northeast tip of the Scottish mainland by the Pentland Firth, the rugged Orkney Islands straddle the Atlantic Ocean and the North Sea. The archipelago consists of some seventy islands, a few of which have been inhabited for six thousand years. The Orkneys lie within Scapa Flow, an eight-hundred-square-mile (2,072 sq. km) inland sea. With an average depth of about sixty-five feet (19.8m), Scapa Flow provides a natural deep-water anchorage. The harbor's strategic location had

been acknowledged at least since the early nineteenth century, and attempts to control passage through Scapa Flow resulted in some of the shipwrecks that remain there to this day.

Two Martello towers still standing on the island of Hoy attest to Scapa Flow's strategic importance. During the War of 1812 British ships often sailed north and west through the Pentland Firth to avoid French privateers instead of using the English Channel. When the United States declared war on Great Britain, the towers were built to protect this northern route: their height enabled Great Britain to protect itself by eliminating the enemy's ability to surprise and offering an advantage if Great Britain did have to fire, though the country managed to defend the area without firing a shot.

In World War I defenses at Scapa Flow were further fortified. As a barrier to German submarines, twenty-one vessels

were intentionally sunk as "blockships" and anti-sub nets were laid. The efforts could not save the HMS *Hampshire*, which sank in 1916 after striking a mine. Lord Kitchener, Minister of War, went down with the ship. Later that year the German fleet faced the British navy off Denmark in the Battle of Jutland, the war's only major naval battle. Although some historians consider the encounter a German defeat, others call it a draw that challenged Britain's previously unquestioned supremacy on the high seas. For the German fleet, the remainder of World War I was relatively uneventful.

DEADLINE FORCES A DECISION

The German fleet had been held at Scapa Flow since November 1918. Virtually prisoners of war, the crews were

unable to go ashore, and marine growth began to take hold on the unmoving hulls. The German government refused to sign the terms of peace that were unveiled in May 1919. The deadline for the German surrender was set for June 21, 1919, at noon.

On the morning of June 21 the British squadron that had been guarding the fleet left Scapa Flow to participate in naval exercises. The Germans believed that the British were making room for reinforcements in case the treaty was not signed. Just before 11 A.M. Admiral von Reuter raised a signal flag to set his plan in motion. Seacocks were opened and seawater pipes were smashed. As a group of schoolchildren on a harbor tour watched from a ferry, the ships began to sink.

The first to go was the twenty-five-thousand-ton (22,700,000kg) Kaiser-class *Freiderich der Grosse*, which slipped

Top: In 1916, the HMS *Hampshire* struck a mine laid by a German submarine that had eluded the first set of "blockships" sunken to guard the harbor. Above: German Commander Gunther Prien salutes as the chief of the U-Boat Division commends the U-47 crew for sinking the *Royal Oak.*

Top: The German battle cruiser *Seydlitz* "turns turtle," rolling upside down before sinking in Scapa Flow. Four cruisers were scuttled in approximately 100 feet (30.5m) of water. Above: Later salvaged by the Royal Navy, the German ship *Hindenburg* came to rest in shallow water.

beneath the surface around 1 P.M. In the next two hours, another fifty-one ships sank completely; the others were beached or saved by the Royal Navy. The German sailors climbed into lifeboats and were picked up on shore by British marines. The HMS *Royal Oak* carried the sailors to the mainland, where they were taken to prison camp before being processed back to Germany.

Ironically, the scuttling made it easier for Germany to sign the peace treaty, as the disposition of its ships was no longer an issue.

A SECOND WORLD WAR, A SECOND SINKING

Throughout the 1920s and 1930s the Orcadians salvaged many of the German ships and sold the metal for scrap. Some of the vessels that

had "turned turtle" and were lying upside down on the bottom were filled with compressed air and floated to the surface. Several of the ships were too deep for salvage. The twenty-five-thousand-ton (22,700,000kg) battleships *König*, *Markgraf*, and *Kronprinz Wilhelm*, plus four fifty-five-hundred-ton (4,994,000kg) cruisers—*Brummer*, *Karlsruhe*, *Dresden*, and *Köln*—and at least four destroyers remained beneath the waters of the harbor. By 1939 most salvage efforts had ceased as Great Britain found itself once again at war with Germany. And once again, the Germans would come to Scapa Flow.

A DARING ATTACK IN THE DEAD OF NIGHT

Built in 1914, the battleship HMS *Royal Oak* was the flagship of the British Navy. The *Royal Oak* carried a crew of one thousand and boasted two gun turrets, each with four fifteen-inch (38.1cm)

What were at one time weapons of war now provide shelter for seagulls. Visitors will find many vestiges of Scapa Flow's wartime past scattered throughout the Orkney's.

cannons, and a speed of twenty knots. On the evening of October 13, 1939, the *Royal Oak*'s crew had every reason to believe that the battleship was safe behind the barricade of blockships that guarded the entrances to Scapa Flow.

But that night German Commander Gunther Prien slipped his U-47 through the channel at Kirk Sound, running on the surface to avoid the blockships. At 1 A.M., as the Northern Lights illuminated the moonless sky, the submarine fired two torpedoes at its target. A second round followed. Fifteen minutes later the *Royal Oak* sank, taking 833 crewmen to the bottom.

Prien returned to Germany, where he was personally decorated by Hitler. The Royal Navy sank twenty more blockships in Scapa Flow, and Winston Churchill, then First Lord of the Admiralty, ordered causeways built for additional protection. Later in the war, the U-47 was sunk by a British destroyer.

BENEATH COLD SEAS

Today a green marker buoy floats above the remains of the *Royal Oak*, which is an official war grave. The wreck lies at a depth of one hundred feet (30.5m), and it still leaks diesel fuel. Following the sinking, two of the ship's cannons were salvaged and put to use aboard the HMS *Abercrombie* and the HMS *Roberts*. Divers also recovered the *Royal Oak*'s bell, which was placed in St. Magnus Cathedral in Kirkwall to commemorate those who were lost in the tragedy. The remains of the torpedo that hit the battleship are in the Stromness Museum in Orkney.

As they did in the 1920s, Orcadians continue to earn an income from the wrecks in Scapa Flow. Since 1980 scuba divers have come to touch history, exploring the area's approximately eighty charted wrecks. Although the *Royal Oak* is off-limits, divers can visit a U-boat, the blockships, and several Royal Navy wrecks. And sitting intact and upright, the World War I ships of the German High Seas Fleet are an impressive sight—a mute testament to a nation's fierce pride.

CHAPTER TWELVE

THE PACIFIC WAR

A CLASH OF TITANS LEAVES CASUALTIES ACROSS THE VAST OCEAN

Kimiou Aisek was searching for killer starfish when instead he found ghosts from his youth. The dark shadow that Aisek discovered in the waters of Truk Lagoon during the 1960s was actually the remains of the *Yamagiri Maru*, one of dozens of Japanese ships sunk in an Allied air strike on this western Pacific atoll on February 17 and 18, 1944. When he was seventeen Aisek had witnessed the attack and suffered the loss of one of his friends, who was a sailor on the *Aikoku Maru*, also sunk in the air raid.

The sky was still dark when the first bombs fell on Truk. Flames licked the surface of the water as wave after wave of fighter planes and dive bombers attacked, and fuel and munitions aboard the vessels in the harbor ignited. Following violent explosions, ships disappeared in clouds of thick, black smoke. Grumman Avengers, American planes, loaded with incendiary and fragmentation bombs cratered airstrips,

At Truk Lagoon, gas masks staring silently from the sediment inside the *Shinkoku Maru* are among the many artifacts that put a human face on the widespread war in the Pacific.

and Japanese planes were destroyed before they could leave the ground.

The Japanese had occupied Truk (now called Chuuk) in the Eastern Caroline Islands since receiving control of the atoll from Germany in 1914. Surrounded by 140 miles (225.3km) of coral reef with only a few channels for passage, this deep-water harbor came to be known as the Gibraltar of the Pacific. Japan closed the islands to outsiders in 1920, and by World War II Truk had become the key outpost of the Japanese Imperial Navy—which had dominated the Pacific from December 1941 until summer 1942. After the Battle of

Above: Batteries sit on shelves inside the five hundred-foot (152.4m) long naval tanker. Right: A clip of machine gun bullets from the forward hold of the _Sankisan Maru_, which rests in shallow water five hundred yards (457.2m) from shore.

Midway the tide began to turn as the Allies developed their own strongholds.

Surprise was a key element of success in the Japanese attack on the U.S. Navy base at Pearl Harbor, and it was this tactic that the Allies used against the Japanese at Truk. Originally planned for April, the mid-February strike on Truk, code-named Operation Hailstorm, was authorized by Admiral Chester Nimitz,

who sent three carrier groups under Vice Admiral Raymond Spruance. Led by Spruance's flagship, the battleship *New Jersey*, the groups launched the attack from a site approximately ninety-five miles (152.9km) east-northeast of Dublon, Truk's largest island.

The early morning invasion achieved its desired outcome, although the mission itself may not have taken the Japanese totally by surprise. Earlier in the month Admiral Mineichi Koga had spotted a reconnaissance plane in the sky over Truk. Suspecting an imminent attack, Koga left the atoll with his flagship the *Mushashi*, four carriers, and several cargo ships, and headed to Palau. Still, the timing and relentlessness of the strike stunned the defenders, who never recovered. Operation Hailstorm successfully neutralized the Japanese base at Truk, damaging or destroying hundreds of enemy aircraft and crippling more than 220,000 tons (199,760,000kg) of Japanese shipping. More than forty vessels lay at the bottom of the lagoon.

Left: The decaying superstructure of the transport ship *Fujikawa Maru* has an eerie beauty. Above: On the *Nippo Maru*, the telegraph which once sent signals to the cargo carrier's engine room stands silent, its once-gleaming brass now covered with colorful corals and gorgonians.

SAVING REEFS
LEADS TO FINDING WRECKS

The ghost fleet remained undisturbed for two decades. Then in the 1960s the Fisheries Department trained Kimiou Aisek and other Trukese to dive for crown-of-thorns starfish (*Acanthaster planci*), which were destroying native reefs by eating the coral. While searching for these voracious echinoderms, Aisek found the *Yamagiri Maru*, a thirty-two-hundred-ton (2,905,600kg) armed freighter lying intact on its port side in 110 feet (33.5m) of water west of the island of Fefan. The vessel was carrying a cargo of eighteen-inch (45.7cm) cannon shells destined for the battleships *Yamato* and *Musashi*. Pilots from the *Bunker Hill*, the *Yorktown*, and the *Enterprise* all reported hits on a ship in that location. Although one of the *Yamagiri*'s holds shows signs of severe damage, it is not known exactly which of the planes might have dealt the fatal blow.

Aisek soon built a business around locating Truk's shipwrecks. At the urging of underwater cinematographer Al Giddings and other pioneers in the then-

Above: Most easily accessible human remains have been removed from the lagoon, but some are still trapped within the wreckage, such as this skull on the *Shinkoku Maru*. Visitors to the site must dive with a guide, and removal of any artifacts is forbidden. Below: A small tank resides 115 feet (35.1m) under water on the deck of the *Nippo Maru*.

fledgling sport, Aisek opened a small dive shop. He provided boats and guides to take visitors to the wreck sites scattered throughout the lagoon. Aisek and his crews found the majority of Truk's wrecks in the 1970s, but vessels are still being located. A destroyer was found in 1987, and in 1994 a Vancouver film crew using sidescan sonar spotted the freighter *Katsuragisan Maru* sitting upright in two hundred feet (61m) of water. In order to protect wreck-related tourism, which brings a few thousand visitors to the islands each year, the government passed strict rules forbidding the removal of any artifacts from the wrecks.

Today, as in the early days of diving in the lagoon, the Trukese guides locate the wrecks by lining up landmarks on the surrounding islands. Some of the vessels, like the freighters *Gosei Maru* and *Sankisan Maru*, are within a few feet (1m) of the surface, and are covered with a pastel blanket of colorful soft corals. The *Gosei* was badly damaged in the attack, and visiting divers can now swim through gaping holes in the small coastal freighter's jumbled remains. The *Sankisan*'s stern is gone, but the bow sits upright and intact, with the port anchor chain stretching out into the sand. The foremast breaks the surface during low tide. The forward cargo hold is full

Above: Cargo aboard the Japanese ships moored at Truk ranges from mundane office supplies, like ink bottles, to munitions and other equipment of war. Right: On one of the many vessels that divers can penetrate in Truk, a companionway leads to an upper deck.

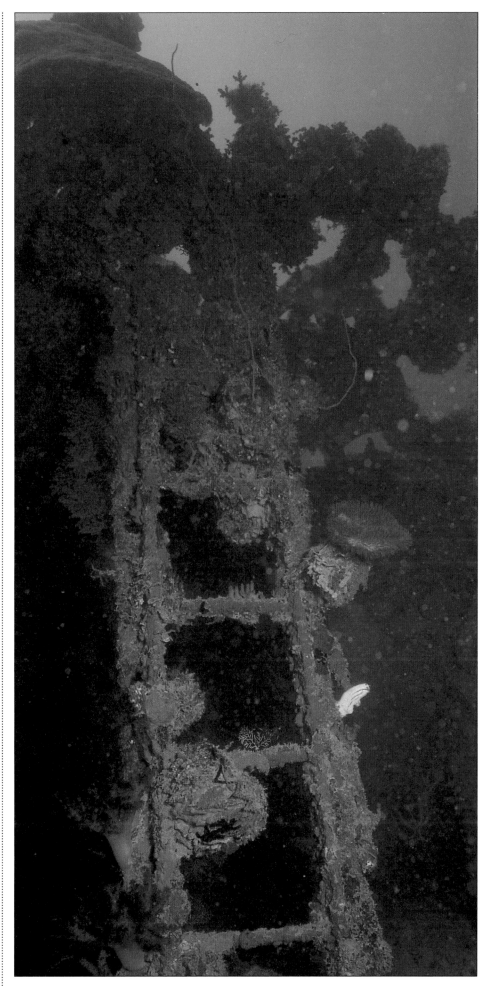

of rifle-caliber ammunition, some spilling out of broken cases and some in machine-gun clips. *Sankisan* also carried two trucks as deck cargo and one in number two hold. Nearly three hundred depth charges were removed from the wreck in the 1970s, but most of the cargo remains on the ship—some corroded after fifty years in Davy Jones's locker, some covered with algae and other marine growth, and some of it clearly recognizable.

Top: Divers can swim along intact passage-ways where soldiers once walked on many of the ships at Truk. Left: A Mitsubishi G4M, nicknamed a "Betty" bomber, lies off Truk's Eten Island.

Exposed to saltwater, iron and steel items like the truck bodies corrode, weaken, and crumble. These artifacts become progressively more fragile and eventually collapse. Brass fittings and fixtures, however, such as the bridge telegraph on the *Nippo Maru*, as well as lanterns and portholes on many of the ships, do not deteriorate, although they may become encrusted with coral and sponges. Similarly, glass sake bottles and china dishes, if undisturbed, will remain for generations. More porous materials such as paper will break down much more slowly under water than they would if they were brought to the surface without painstaking preservation techniques. Even after all this time visitors to Truk can still find books, shoes, uniforms, and other personal items strewn amongst the wreckage.

DEEPER SECRETS

Only occasionally will divers see human remains. According to the Shinto religion the souls of those who die in battle linger in limbo until the soldiers' remains are attended to with the proper ceremonies. Trukese divers have been paid well to recover any accessible human remains and return them to the Japanese. From time to time on the shallower wrecks a guide will show a diver a skull or a bone that has been well hidden, but for the most part remains on these wrecks have been removed. On deeper wrecks that lie near the operational limits of scuba divers breathing compressed air, this is not always the case. In 1984 skeletal remains were removed from one hold of the troop transport vessel *Aikoku Maru*, which rests in more than two hundred feet (61m) of water. The cremated ashes were transported to Tokyo, where they were scattered at sea following religious ceremonies at Japan's Tomb of the Unknown Soldier. The *Aikoku* carried more than four hundred soldiers, and those who perished deep inside the ship may lie there still.

At these depths water filters out most colors of the spectrum, leaving everything awash in shades of blue and indigo. Coral growth is less prolific due to the lack of light, leaving the vessel's graceful lines clearly visible. Built as a passenger liner and conscripted to carry men and munitions, the *Aikoku* sits upright as if she were steaming across

Commissioned in 1916, the USS *Arizona* was a Pennsylvania-class battleship. She was modernized in 1929, and was scheduled for repairs in early December 1941.

the sand bottom. Her bow, forward of the bridge, is missing, having been vaporized by one or more of the five-hundred-pound (227kg) bombs that struck it. Observers on shore felt the force of the concussion, which knocked an Allied plane out of the sky. Today, in contrast to the chaos of Operation Hailstorm, the *Aikoku* sits in eerie silence. Inside the bridge, nestled in a deep layer of silt, withered wreaths of flowers rest beside a human skull. The flowers are a tribute to Kimiou Aisek's friend and all the others who died in the Hailstorm over Truk Lagoon.

MUTE MEMORIALS THROUGHOUT THE PACIFIC

Truk Lagoon may be the largest graveyard of ships from World War II, but it is not the only one. The ocean whose name means "peaceful" holds numerous skeletons of warships and planes that were downed in the conflict. Among the best known

U.S.S. ARIZONA

is the battleship USS *Arizona*, one of eighteen warships sunk or damaged during the attack on Pearl Harbor, which drew the United States into war against Japan in December 1941. More than a million and a half people a year visit the *Arizona* memorial in Honolulu to pay their respects to the 1,177 officers and crewmen who were lost when a bomb hit the vessel's forward magazine in the first minutes of the early-morning attack. The names of the fallen are engraved in marble inside the memorial building spanning the *Arizona*'s shattered hull, which lies in shallow enough water to be seen from the surface.

Ninety-six warships were anchored or dry-docked in Pearl Harbor on the day of

Top: Eight bomb hits, including one that struck the ship's forward magazine, doomed the *Arizona*, which burned for two days. Right: This 1954 aerial photograph shows the *Arizona* as she looked prior to the construction of the memorial that spans her remains.

the attack. There would have been more, but heavy weather delayed the carrier USS *Enterprise* and its escorts, which were supposed to have arrived in Honolulu on December 6. At the end of the two-hour strike the U.S. Navy and Marines had lost a total of 2,113 troops, and nearly a thousand more were wounded. For six months

following the bombing of Pearl Harbor, Japan ruled the Pacific.

THE SUMMER OF '42

With the exception of the *Arizona*, the *Utah*, and the *Oklahoma*, the battleships

that were attacked in Pearl Harbor were salvaged and soon saw action in the Pacific. The Battle of Midway in June 1942 was pivotal. Although outnumbered, U.S. forces sank four Japanese carriers within twenty-four hours, forcing the Japanese Imperial Navy to suffer its first major defeat in 450 years.

The following month the Japanese began construction of an airfield on Guadalcanal in the Solomon Islands in the southwestern Pacific. In August the Americans launched an amphibious counteroffensive, capturing the airstrip and preventing the Japanese from resupplying their thirty-six thousand troops on the island. Over the next six months the two sides fought for control over the strategic airfield. The conflict climaxed in a bloody naval battle that began during a downpour on the night of November 11. Among the numerous casualties were the transport vessel *Hirokawa Maru*, the Japanese submarine I-123, the tanker USS *Kanawa*, the light cruiser USS *Atlanta*, two U.S. troop transports, and a B-17 bomber. So many vessels were lost on both sides that the waters north of Guadalcanal earned the nickname Iron Bottom Sound.

A few of the vessels at Guadalcanal were run aground so they could be unloaded before they sank, but most rest in

Left: A sailor climbs the gun turrets on the stricken USS *Oklahoma*'s canted deck. One of eight battleships at Pearl Harbor on the day of the attack, the vessel capsized after taking three torpedo hits. Above: The *Oklahoma* was eventually refloated in 1944 and removed from the harbor.

deep water. In 1992 oceanographer Dr. Robert Ballard explored Iron Bottom Sound using submersibles and remotely operated vehicles. Three years later divers Terrence Tysall and Kevin Denlay became the first people to touch the wreck of the USS *Atlanta*, in four hundred feet (122m) of water, since she was sent to the bottom. They left behind a plaque that reads, in part:

"We are privileged to visit and touch your grave with the utmost reverence, asking those that follow to preserve this spirit. May we all learn from your struggle. May your battles never be forgotten."

FRIENDLY FIRE

After being hit by two torpedoes, the stunned *Atlanta* had stumbled into "friendly fire" from the heavy cruiser USS *San Francisco*. When it was obvious that the stricken ship could not be saved, she was scuttled.

A month earlier the *President Coolidge* sank as a result of "friendly fire" of a different sort. In October 1942, the former passenger liner was carrying five thousand troops and supplies to the U.S. Marine outpost at Guadalcanal. En route, the vessel headed to the island of Espiritu Santo in Vanuatu, about six hundred miles (965.4km) east of the Solomons. When Captain Henry Nelson approached Luganville Harbor the radio operator on the island tried frantically to warn him away, but just as the message came through, the *Coolidge* struck first one then another of the mines laid to protect the harbor.

Captain Nelson ran the *Coolidge* aground on a ledge and gave the order to abandon ship. A few hours later the vessel slipped off her precarious perch on the sand ledge and disappeared. Only two lives were lost—one in the initial explosion and one during the evacuation.

The *Coolidge* came to rest on her port side, her bow in about seventy feet (21.3m) of water a short swim from the beach. Today the wreck's location is

Above: Launched in 1931, the *President Coolidge* carried passengers between San Francisco and the Orient for a decade before she was converted to a troop transport in 1941. Right: Nearly all of the more than five thousand soldiers and crew members aboard the *Coolidge* were rescued in the two hours between when the ship struck a mine and when she disappeared beneath the Pacific waters.

A photograph taken just after the *President Coolidge* slipped off the reef and into the sea shows hundreds of survivors of the former five million dollar luxury liner swimming and boating safely to shore.

marked by a buoy. At 654 feet (199.3m) long, the vessel is perhaps the largest wreck from the Second World War—and one of the largest from any era—that is accessible to scuba divers. A cargo of Jeeps and airplane fuel tanks, as well as office furnishings, speak to the *Coolidge*'s role as a war machine, as do a deck gun on the bow. Rifle clips and gas masks further remind visitors of the nature of the vessel's final mission. Yet other sights—a swimming pool, an elegant tiled fountain, an Elizabethan lady carved above the fireplace in the main salon—provide a glimpse of happier times, when the *President Coolidge* carried well-to-do passengers across a more peaceful Pacific Ocean.

COLD-WAR CASUALTIES

The atomic bombs dropped on the Japanese cities of Hiroshima and Nagasaki in early August 1945 effectively ended the war in the Pacific. On September 2, Japanese representatives signed a formal document of surrender aboard the battleship USS *Missouri* in Tokyo Bay.

The fighting was over, but the bombing wasn't—nor were the ship sinkings. During atomic bomb tests at Bikini Atoll in the Marshall Islands, at least fourteen ships were sent to the bottom. Under Operation Crossroads in July 1946 seventy ships and submarines were brought to Bikini for a study of the impact on naval vessels of an atomic explosion similar in force to the blast at Nagasaki. They included obsolete U.S. warships, as well as vessels captured from Japan and Germany. All were still fully armed and outfitted for war. Test animals took the place of crew.

Forty-two thousand servicemen watched from outside the reef as "Able" was detonated above water on July 1, and five ships sank. Later that month "Baker" was set off beneath the surface, bringing down nine more vessels. In the days that followed, nine of the ships that remained on the surface were scuttled, and servicemen scrubbed the decks of the others in an attempt to remove the radiation. Among those ships now lying at the bottom of the lagoon are Admiral William Frederick "Bull" Halsey's flagship, the aircraft carrier *Saratoga*, a veteran of battles at Iwo Jima and Guadalcanal. The *Saratoga* survived five kamikaze strikes in a single day only to meet her end as a guinea pig for a new weapon of war. Lying upside down in the same lagoon is the *Nagato*, from whose decks Admiral Isoroku Yamamoto launched the attack on Pearl Harbor that marked the beginning of war in the Pacific.

A Japanese troop transport, a casualty of the battle fought in November 1942, rests sunk by the stern off the beach at Guadalcanal.

CHAPTER THIRTEEN

THE ANDREA DORIA

A "FLOATING ART GALLERY" FASCINATES ADVENTURE SEEKERS

The luxury liner *Andrea Doria* had barely been on the ocean bottom a day before she had visitors from the sunlit world above the surface. Department store heir Peter Gimbel and Joseph Fox were the first to visit the opulently appointed vessel's final resting place, in 240 feet (73.2m) of water sixty-five miles (104.6km) south of Nantucket Island, just off the northeastern seaboard of the United States. They returned with photographs that graced the pages of *LIFE* magazine. In the forty-odd years since, others have followed, although never in great numbers. By most estimates fewer than five hundred people have visited the wreck; at least seven of those have died. A long way from shore, and at depths considered unsafe for scuba divers, the *Andrea Doria* is difficult to reach. Currents and conditions can quickly become hostile and blue sharks often cruise the surrounding waters. Its inaccessibility is part of the appeal. The level of skill and daring necessary to dive the wreck, coupled with the notoriety of the ship's sinking and the subsequent rescue at sea of nearly seventeen hundred passengers, has attracted adventurers like Gimbel and others. For scuba divers the *Andrea Doria* has earned a reputation as the Mount Everest of shipwrecks.

A PICTURE-PERFECT PASSENGER LINER

Named after a sixteenth-century Genoese admiral and statesman, the *Andrea Doria* was launched in 1951 by the Italian Line. The seven-hundred-foot-long (213.4m) vessel was lavishly decorated with specially commissioned works by some of Italy's finest living artists, and it was touted as "a floating art gallery." A massive mural by Salvatore Fuimi in the ship's First Class Lounge paid tribute to Raphael, Michelangelo, and other masters of Italy's artistic heritage. Outside the lounge stood a life-size bronze statue of Admiral Andrea Doria, donated by a descendent. Over its head, in silver, hung a replica of the family crest. Ceramic panels by Guido Gambone and Romano Rui graced the ship. The chapel, with its original frescoes and Romanesque columns, was a study in Gothic elegance.

One of the most dramatic sinkings in recent memory occurred when the passenger liners the *Andrea Doria* and the *Stockholm* collided off the coast of Nantucket hours before the Doria was due to arrive in New York.

Deluxe first-class suites were decorated by the finest designers.

The *Andrea Doria* had accommodations for 1,241 passengers and 575 crew. First, cabin, and tourist class each had their own swimming pools and dining areas. The ship provided service from Genoa, Italy, to New York City at a cruising speed of twenty-three knots. When the pride of the Italian Line left Italy on July 7, 1956, with Captain Piero Calamai at her helm, the *Andrea Doria* had made one hundred Atlantic crossings without incident.

TWO SHIPS IN THE NIGHT

The ship cruised the Riviera, then passed through the Strait of Gibraltar and into the Atlantic Ocean. She was due to arrive in New York early on the morning of July 26. The passengers amused themselves with sunbathing and shuffleboard, walking along the open Promenade Deck, and other pastimes.

The *Andrea Doria* was quiet on Wednesday evening, July 25, as she approached the Nantucket Lightship.

With just a few hours before the ship made port, many passengers packed their belongings. Despite a thick blanket of fog that limited visibility to a half mile (805m) or less, Captain Calamai was running at just under twenty-two knots in order to stay on schedule.

At approximately 10:20 P.M. the *Andrea Doria* passed about a mile (1.6km) south of the lightship, a navigational aid in an area sometimes called the "Times Square of the Atlantic" due to heavy shipping traffic moving to and

from New York Harbor. The liner was headed due west.

At 10:45 P.M. a ship appeared on the *Andrea Doria*'s radar screen. Seventeen miles (27.4km) away, the ship was traveling east toward the liner. It was an unexpected sight, as vessels leaving New York usually followed a sea lane much farther south than the one used by inbound ships. The other ship was the passenger liner *Stockholm*.

Ordinarily, two ships approaching each other pass port-to-port—that is, with their left sides facing—unless moving into such a position would cause them to cross paths. The blip on the *Andrea Doria*'s radar screen appeared as though it would pass several miles off the liner's starboard side. To ensure a wider gap between the two ships, Calamai ordered the *Andrea Doria* turned slightly to port. Aboard the *Stockholm* the radar showed an approaching ship that would pass on the Swedish liner's port side.

When the officers on the *Andrea Doria*'s bridge spotted the *Stockholm*'s running lights, the Swedish ship was headed toward them. Instead of facing the *Stockholm* head on to present the smallest target, Captain Calamai attempted to avoid a collision altogether. He ordered the *Andrea Doria* turned hard to port and tried to outrun the oncoming ship. All he succeeded in doing was turning the *Andrea Doria* broadside.

At 11:10 P.M. the *Stockholm*'s bow, reinforced for the icy North Atlantic waters, sliced through the *Andrea Doria*'s

Left: Once news of the collision reached New York, news photographers flocked to the site to document the *Doria*'s last hours. In this photograph she heels to starboard. Above: Debris floats away from the wreckage as the liner slips bow-first beneath the Atlantic Ocean.

starboard side, penetrating thirty feet (9.1m) into the ship and crushing cabins on five decks. Forty-six *Andrea Doria* passengers and six crewmen on the *Stockholm* were killed. Later both parties would claim that the other turned into its path. The issue was settled out of court, and no explanation was ever made public.

RESCUE AT SEA

With seawater pouring in over her bulkheads, the *Andrea Doria* began to list heavily. Although the ship carried more than enough lifeboats for all those on board, the sinking ship's steep cant made half of them unlaunchable. An S.O.S. went out and was picked up by several vessels at 11:22 P.M.

Although its bow was broken off in the collision, the *Stockholm* remained afloat and picked up some of the *Andrea Doria*'s pas-sengers. One of those rescues was a lucky accident: a little girl sleeping in one of the *Andrea Doria*'s starboard cabins was cata-pulted onto the retreating *Stockholm*, where she was discovered amidst a pile of wreck-age. Her parents assumed that she was dead until the wounded liner limped into New York port nearly two days later, and she was found.

The nearby freighter *Cape Ann* and the navy transport vessel *Pvt. William H. Thomas* picked up as many survivors as they could. The liner *Ile de France* was two hours beyond the sinking site on its way to Europe when it picked up the *Andrea Doria*'s distress call. Her captain turned the ship around and doubled its speed. By dawn she had picked up the last of the *Andrea Doria*'s passengers. News photographers captured the event on film. The final shot of the *Andrea Doria*, showing part of the stern hull and one propeller, was taken at 10:10 A.M. on July 26, 1956.

Above: Divers have recovered a wide range of artifacts from the *Doria*, including this decorative ceramic panel by artist Guido Gambone. Opposite: The *Stockholm* sits in dry-dock at the Bethlehem Steel yard in Brooklyn, New York, awaiting repair.

THE LURE OF LUXURY

Peter Gimbel's obsession with the *Andrea Doria* began almost immediately. His black-and-white photos taken the day after the sinking illustrated a *LIFE* magazine article on the event written by *Titanic* authority Walter Lord. Two weeks later Gimbel returned to the wreck to shoot color photographs for a second *LIFE* story entitled "Daring Divers Inside *Andrea Doria*," which ran in the September 17, 1956 issue.

Gimbel returned to the wreck sev-eral times over the next two decades. Other professional dive teams did too, including cinematographer Frederic Dumas and cameraman Louis Malle. In 1964 a group of former commercial and navy divers salvaged the bronze statue of Andrea Doria, which is now in a banquet hall in a Florida hotel. Docu-mentaries were filmed at the site in 1968 and 1975.

In 1981, Gimbel mounted his most ambitious expedition yet, spending the entire month of August on the *Andrea Doria* with a team of saturation divers. To maximize efficiency, saturation divers spend several hours a day working on the wreck, then return to "live" in a chamber that is pressurized to their working depth. Instead of decompres-sing after each dive, they decompress once at the end of the project. In addi-tion to generating film for another docu-mentary, Gimbel's team had a second goal: to salvage the ship's safe. Despite hostile weather and many setbacks, the divers shot more than fifty hours of film. They also recovered the Bank of Rome safe, which was deposited for safekeep-ing in the Coney Island (New York) Aquarium's shark tank until the docu-mentary was completed, so that no one would dare steal the recovered treasure.

The documentary aired in August 1984. Part of the program, broadcast live

from Coney Island, featured Gimbel and his wife Elga Anderson opening the safe. Inside were bundles of soggy Italian lire, some of which were later separated, mounted in acrylic, and sold as souvenirs. The safe can still be seen at the aquarium.

FOR THE LOVE OF ADVENTURE

Over the years other groups of divers also visited the *Andrea Doria*. They were amateurs in the truest sense of the word—highly skilled, but unpaid for their efforts, they researched and explored the wreck out of passion. Some took photographs of the once-elegant ship, now covered with sea anemones and draped with trawler nets. Others gathered souvenirs. China and crystal from the dining rooms, bearing the Italia logo, are prized mementos. In the late 1960s, using equipment that is crude by today's standards, John Dudas of Passaic, New Jersey retrieved the brass compass from the ship's bridge, which was still intact at the time. The bridge has since collapsed and lies in ruins on the sea floor. Dudas was diving with his future wife Evelyn Bartram, who was the first woman to dive the *Andrea Doria*. Taking advantage of increasingly sophisticated scuba equipment, including submersible computers and diver propulsion vehicles, she continues to dive the wreck to this day.

There were others—each with a unique relationship with the wreck. Steve Gatto, an electrician from New Jersey, recovered an auxiliary helm and a brass-framed window pane from the Promenade Deck. Bill Campbell, an insurance salesman from Rhode Island, and Steve Bielenda, a dive-boat captain from Long Island, placed a commemorative plaque on the wreck to mark the twenty-fifth anniversary of the sinking. After making a number of dives on the *Andrea Doria*, a pharmaceutical clinical scientist named David Bright organized an annual reunion dinner for survivors of the disaster. Another group of enthusiasts organized by boat captain Bill Nagle salvaged the ship's stern bell. Making only one dive a day it took six divers, working in teams of two for about twenty minutes at a time, five days at the site to locate the bell and rig it so that it could be brought to the surface.

A seventh person on the bell salvage expedition was John Moyer, who did not participate in any of the dives because he had been struck with decompression sickness just two weeks earlier. He worked in the business office of a southern New Jersey pharmacy, but lived

Now immersed in sea life, a bathroom in the *Doria's* first-class passenger area hints at the opulence that once surrounded passengers on the celebrated liner. Today, many areas inside the ship are full of loose cables and debris, and the wreck's orientation makes safe navigation of its passages difficult.

Inside a stairwell, divers discovered a large stack of china from the second-class dining room. Each of the three passenger classes of the *Doria* had its own china pattern.

for the Grande Dame of the Sea, which he first dived in 1981, and had an extensive collection of *Andrea Doria* memorabilia. In 1993, Moyer filed an admiralty "arrest" on the wreck, a legal procedure that essentially grants him ownership of the vessel and its contents, basically because he was the first to stake an official salvage claim. His primary interest was that he be able to explore the bow area undisturbed in hopes of finding the *Andrea Doria*'s bow bell. He has yet to bring back that prize, but he has recovered other treasures. The most spectacular among them are two seven-

hundred-pound (317.8kg) architectural dividers from the ship's Winter Garden Lounge. The five-by six-foot (1.5 by 1.8m) panels feature mosaics by Guido Gambone, a ceramic artist.

Six other panels—two of them twenty-five feet (7.6m) long—remain on the wreck. To reach them divers will have to navigate dark waters through the disorienting corridors of a ship that is lying on its side. They will have to work without stirring up the fine silt that settles over everything inside the wreck. And they will spend twenty minutes descending and working their way inside, then more

than ninety minutes surfacing, in order to avoid potentially paralyzing decompression illness (the bends). All the while, they'll live at sea on a small boat, killing the long hours in between dives with fishing for blue sharks and telling stories—of the *Andrea Doria*, of other wrecks they've seen, and of wrecks they have yet to explore.

CHAPTER FOURTEEN

THE EDMUND FITZGERALD

A GREAT LAKES TRAGEDY LIVES ON IN SONG AND LOVED ONES' MEMORIES

The *Edmund Fitzgerald*'s brass bell rang as it had rung to mark the passing of each half-hour in its seventeen years of service. But this time each resonant note marked the passing of a life in the ship's tragic sinking twenty years earlier. As families of the crewmen mourned, the bell rang twenty-nine times. Then it tolled once more for all those who have lost their lives on the Great Lakes.

The sand-cast bell had been a point of pride among the *Fitzgerald*'s crew, who polished it daily to keep its brass gleaming. When it was retrieved from the wreck in a high-tech operation in the summer of 1995, it was covered with a layer of black sulfide and corrosion from the iron bell stand. Conservators tried to clean it with baking soda, then lemon juice, and finally resorted to formic acid. Further soaking, scrubbing, and power washing was necessary to remove the wet, red substance that weeped from the bell—possibly iron oxides from ore dust that the brass may have absorbed. The letters spelling out

Below: The stern of the *Edmund Fitzgerald* lies more than five hundred feet (152.4m) below the surface of Lake Superior. Right: During a 1994 expedition, a research vessel from the Harbor Branch Oceanographic Institution lowers a submersible into the waters of Lake Superior.

the *Edmund Fitzgerald*'s name were repainted black, as they had been when the ore carrier plied the Great Lakes, and the bell was polished and lacquered. Following the commemorative ceremony, the *Fitzgerald*'s bell was placed in a memorial to the crew at the Great Lakes Shipwreck Museum at Whitefish Point, Michigan, seventeen miles (27.4km) from where the *Fitzgerald* sank in Lake Superior. In the original bell's place on the wreck is a replica engraved with the names of the twenty-nine who perished.

THE GALES OF NOVEMBER

Those who sail the inland seas known as the Great Lakes respect the fierce late-autumn winds that sweep across the lake, sometimes forming massive waves. In November 1913 one storm sank eighteen ships and took more than 250 lives on Lake Huron. For that reason

most Great Lakes shipping wraps up for the season in early November. When the *Edmund Fitzgerald* left Silver Bay with twenty-six thousand tons (23,608,000kg) of taconite iron pellets on November 9, 1975, it was to be the 729-foot (222.2m) ore carrier's final run across Lake Superior for the season. Built in the 1950s, the forty-thousand-ton (36,320,000kg) vessel got off to an ominous start. As the ship was being christened, it slipped off its pier, and an observer suffered a fatal heart attack.

However, the morning of the November 9 was warm and calm, with no foreshadowing of the tragedy to come. A veteran with forty-four seasons on the water, Captain Ernest McSorley headed "the Big Fitz" toward Detroit. The route would first take the vessel through Whitefish Bay and the locks at Sault Ste. Marie between Michigan's Upper Peninsula and Canada, then on into Lake Huron. About nine miles (14.5km) behind the *Fitzgerald*, another ore carrier, the *Arthur Anderson*, was making the same journey.

WORSENING WEATHER

Around 6 P.M. McSorley and the *Anderson's* Captain Bernie Cooper discussed the deteriorating weather. To avoid the northeast gale the two vessels headed north to hug the Canadian shoreline. Later that night winds reached sixty miles (96.5km) per hour, with even stronger gusts, and visibility diminished to less than two miles (3.2km). By noon the next day the vessels were sailing in a whiteout, tossed by sixteen-foot (4.9m) waves. Around 3 P.M., McSorley radioed that the *Fitzgerald* had started to list to starboard and its pumps were running. About an

hour later he noted that the wind had snapped the ship's radar masts. The wind continued to howl—sometimes up to eighty-five miles (136.8km) per hour— and the waves continued to build.

A power outage had darkened the lighthouse at Whitefish Point, leaving the ships sailing blind in seas that had increased to twenty-five feet (7.6m) high. At 5 P.M. McSorley radioed Cooper for a position check; McSorley was told that the *Fitzgerald* was a few miles from Whitefish Point.

At 6:30 P.M. two waves thirty-five feet (10.5m) high struck the *Arthur Anderson*.

At 7:10 P.M. the *Anderson* received a radio message from the Big Fitz. "We're holding our own." They were the last words ever heard from the *Edmund Fitzgerald*.

DISAPPEARED

When the *Anderson's* crew next checked their radar screen, they saw no sign of the *Fitzgerald*. Radio messages got no response. Nor did the ship appear a short time later when visibility began to improve. The U.S. Coast Guard, the *Anderson*, and the *William Clay Ford*, another vessel from the harbor in Whitefish Bay, searched all night, but

Left: The "The Big Fitz" slides into a launching basin two months before she is completed in late summer of 1958. With a capacity of twenty-six thousand tons (26,608,000kg), the eight million dollar ore carrier was the largest and longest vessel existing on the Great Lakes at the time. Above: An upside-down lifeboat was one of the few signs of the sunken *Edmund Fitzgerald* that searchers were able to locate.

found only flotsam: half a lifeboat, life preservers and other debris, and an oil slick. The *Edmund Fitzgerald* had vanished with all hands.

The cause of the sinking remains a mystery, although at least three theories have been offered by way of explanation. According to a fifty-page report by the Coast Guard the tragedy was due to "ineffective closure of cargo hatches," which allowed the ship to take on water. Others say that the hatches on ore carriers such as the *Fitzgerald* are heavy enough to seal themselves, even if some of their hatch clamps are not completely tight. Some of those who disagree with the official account think that the *Fitzgerald* suffered the same fate as the *Daniel J. Morrell*, which had bottomed

out on Six Fathom Shoal years earlier, causing a stress fracture that sank the ship. On some charts of the area, they say, Six Fathom Shoal appears a mile (1.6km) east of its actual location. Still others say that the lack of a Mayday call indicates a sudden catastrophe—which might have been the case if one of the huge waves that struck the *Anderson* had pushed the *Fitzgerald*'s bow beneath the lake's surface.

LOOKING DEEPER INTO A LEGEND

The sinking of the *Edmund Fitzgerald* soon became part of Great Lakes lore. Folksinger Gordon Lightfoot immortalized the disaster in song. Lying in two chunks more than five hundred feet (152.4m) below the surface of Lake Superior in Canadian waters seventeen miles (27.4km) north of

Whitefish Point, the wreck has never been far from the consciousness of those who lost friends and loved ones on the ship. Family members were particularly upset when a documentary filmmaker who visited the wreck in 1994 reported finding a body on the bow. According to expedition leader Fred Shannon, crew members aboard a sixteen-foot (4.9m) submersible saw the body as well as personal effects while videotaping the site.

Shannon's expedition to the wreck was not the first. The Coast Guard videotaped the site in 1976, and Jacques Cousteau's team visited the site a few years later. Submersible dives to the *Fitzgerald* were also made as part of the Dive '94: Great Lakes Science Program, a project headed by the Harbor Branch Oceanographic Institution of Fort Pierce, Florida and the MacInnis Foundation, Ontario, Canada. Students in the University of Connecticut Aquanaut Program participated in the expedition, which was part of a two-month study of the Great Lakes ecosystem.

The hydraulic force created when the *Fitzgerald* sank bow-first bent this radio direction finder, which sits atop the pilot house at a depth of 470 feet (143.3m). The ship's bell is in the background.

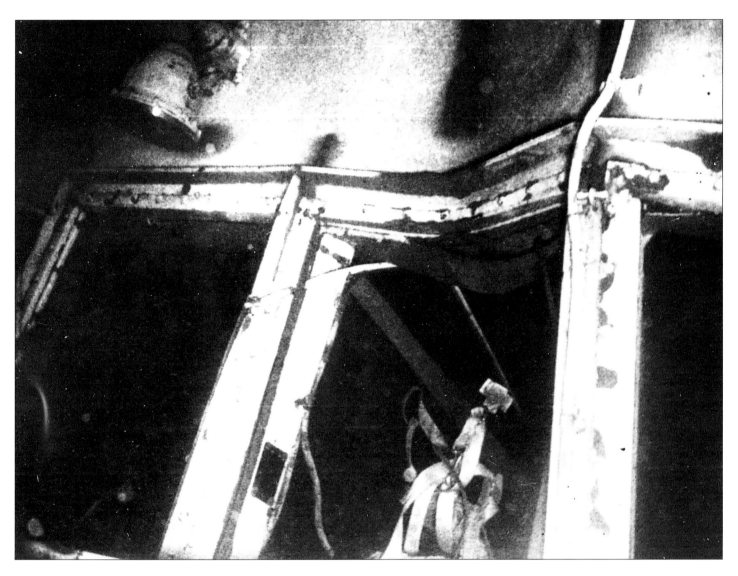

BRINGING BACK THE BELL

The most ambitious expeditions, and most likely the final ones, took place in 1995.

Families of the victims had two requests. First, they asked for a tangible memorial. Second, they asked that no more dives be permitted on the wreck out of respect for the dead.

With permission from the families, the Canadian government, and the ship's owners, a multi-organizational expedition led by Thomas Farnquist of the Great Lakes Historical Society was set for July 1995. Participants included The Discovery Channel and National Geographic. Teams aboard the three-person submersible *Clelia* videotaped the wreck. The 195-pound (88.5kg) bell was retrieved by Canadian diver Bruce Fuoco, who wore a pressurized, aluminum suit called a Newtsuit. The Newtsuit allows divers to explore depths to

twelve hundred feet (365.8m) and return to the surface without need for decompression. In addition to the bell salvage, the expedition resulted in a documentary that traced the ship's history and sinking, and showed the moving dedication ceremony following the bell's recovery.

Two months after the bell was brought to the surface two scuba divers visited the wreck as part of a research project on decompression illness. After two years of planning, Terry Tysall, an oceanography student from Orlando, Florida and his dive partner Mike Zee of Chicago dived to the wreck breathing special mixtures of oxygen, nitrogen, and helium blended for the wreck's extreme depths. It took the divers six minutes to reach the wreck and they could only spend another six minutes on the bottom—barely enough time to touch the ship's handrail. The decom-

Using U.S. Navy cameras, the U.S. Coast Guard captured this image of the *Fitzgerald*'s pilot house during a May 1976 expedition to investigate the cause of the sinking. A lifejacket seen floating through the window is a chilling reminder of the twenty-nine men who were trapped and died when the ship went down.

pression lasted three hours before they could leave the water.

Never before had free-swimming divers visited the 535-foot-deep (163.1m) wreck without high-tech protection, carrying only scuba tanks—and it may not happen again for some time. Tysall and Zee surfaced to criticism from the victims' families. Following their dives the two men contacted many of the lost crewmen's family members in an attempt to explain their motivations. After more than twenty years the wound is still fresh, and healing comes slowly.

CHAPTER FIFTEEN

DISCOVERIES TO COME

MORE STORIES REMAIN TO BE WRITTEN

Three-quarters of the Earth is covered by water, and no one knows how many vessels lie beneath its surface. "Thousands" wouldn't begin to tell the story—even if we limited ourselves to documented sinkings. The number still grows, too, although not at the rate it once did. Despite modern advances in both navigation and marine engineering, vessels still fall victim to weather, shoals, each other, and human carelessness. In recent years another class of wrecks has been added as scuba divers and anglers arrange to sink derelict vessels as artificial reefs. In 1996 ships were sunk for recreational purposes in the Cayman Islands and the British Virgin Islands, and plans for a similar program are under development for the Sea of Cortez.

The number of known shipwrecks will only continue to grow as technology becomes more advanced. Moving a step beyond sonar, tools like sub-bottom profilers enable researchers to find remnants of shipwrecks buried beneath layers of mud and silt. In the last decade engineers have developed equipment that can perform tasks at incredible depths that long lay out of reach. Now sophisticated sonar linked to a research vessel's navigation system can cut search time significantly, increasing both efficiency and the likelihood of success. Still, for the foreseeable future, use of these often-costly technologies is likely to be limited to high-profile projects of significant historic or monetary value.

A diver investigates a Russian destroyer sunk as part of a program to create artificial reefs near the Cayman Islands. Note the bars on the doors to prevent divers from penetrating the wreck.

Free-swimming divers also benefit from improved technology. For example, by breathing gases other than ordinary compressed air, they extend the depths to which they can dive. As pressurized one-atmosphere suits and rebreathers become better and more affordable, they will further expand divers' capabilities. These suits increase the breathing gas supply, allowing access to ships that haven't been touched since the day they sank.

Lower in cost than submersibles, surface-supplied gases, and saturation-diving systems, these free-swimming improvements are the impetus behind research and exploration of many shipwrecks that might be overlooked by academic organizations or commercial salvage interests. One case in point is currently under way off the coast of New Jersey. A group of divers has tentatively identified an unknown WWII German

submarine as the U-869. They have also located at least five of the six ships sunk by the U-151 on a single day in 1918 known as Black Sunday. The group, led by John Chatterton, was granted salvage rights to one of the vessels, the *Carolina*, by a judge whose father came ashore in one of the passenger ship's lifeboats.

As technology continues to evolve, our knowledge of ships and shipwrecks will continue to expand. And shipwrecks will always draw us in—at least some of us. Some may be content to look across the surface of the water and remain oblivious to the voices that call up from beneath. The rest of us will be listening intently to their stories.

Above: Rotting pages found inside a wreck at Truk (above) are all that is left of a logbook dutifully kept by a Japanese soldier. Right: Jars found at the wreck at Bozburun, Turkey, provide key details to learning about daily life in the period when they were used.

SHIPWRECK RESOURCES

Listed below are some sources of ship-wreck information. Other resources to investigate include the National Archives, local historical societies and libraries, as well as specialty publications for divers, anglers, and history enthusiasts.

A Guide to Maritime History on the Internet—http://ils.unc.edu/maritime/home.html

Bateaux Below—P.O. Box 2134, Wilton, NY 12866; ph: 518-587-7638

Center for Maritime and Underwater Research Management—Michigan State University, East Lansing, MI 48824-1047; ph: 517-353-5190

East Carolina University Program in Maritime History and Nautical Archaeo-logy—ECU Dept. of History, Greenville, NC 27858-4353; ph: 919-328-6131; e-mail: webmaster@ecuvm.cis.ecu.edu

The program maintains an index of shipwreck information at: http://ecuvax.cis.ecu.edu/academics/schdept/hist/maritime/maritime.html

Florida State University Directory of Underwater Archaeology on the World Wide Web—http://ocean.fsu.edu/oce/dive/uwdirect.html

Great Lakes Historical Shipwreck Society—110 Whitefish Pt. Rd., Paradise, MI 49768; ph: 906-635-1742

Independence Seaport Museum—211 S. Columbus Blvd., Philadelphia, PA 19106; ph: 215-925-5439

Institute of Nautical Archaeology at Texas A&M University—P.O. Drawer U, College Station, TX 77841-5137; ph: 409-854-6694; email: nautical@tamu.edu

International Treasure Hunters Exchange web site—www.treasure.com

Mariners Museum—100 Museum Dr., Newport News, VA 23606-3759; ph: 804-596-2222; e-mail: info@mariner.org

Maritime History Virtual Archives—http://pc-78-120.udac.se:8001/www/nautica/nautica.html

Monitor National Marine Sanctuary—National Oceanic and Atmospheric Administration (NOAA) Bldg. 1519, Ft. Eustis, VA 23604

National Maritime Historical Society—5 John Walsh Blvd., Peekskill, NY 10566; ph: 718-737-7878

National Maritime Initiative—P.O. Box 37127, Washington, DC, 20013-7127

National Ocean Service—6001 Executive Blvd., Rockville, MD 20852

National Oceanic and Atmospheric Administration (NOAA) Sanctuaries and Reserves Division—1305 East West Hwy., SSMC4-12, Silver Spring, MD 20910; ph: 301-713-3145; web site: http://www.nos.noaa.gov

National Park Service Submerged Cultural Resources Division—P.O. Box 728, Santa Fe, NM 87504-0728

Peabody Museum of Salem—East India Square, Salem, MA 01970; ph: 508-745-9500

Queensland Shipwrecks web site—http://www.ion.com.au/~stevel

One man's dinner dishes (from the *Andrea Doria*) become another's man history lesson beneath the waters of the world, where more artifacts and more stories wait to be uncovered everyday.

Scuba Diving, Great Lakes, and Other Neat Stuff web site—http://www.ourworld.compuserve.com/homepages/PChurch/

Smithsonian Institution, Curator of Naval History—National Museum of American History, Washington, DC 20560

South Street Seaport Museum—207 Front St., New York, NY 10038; ph: 212-669-9475

Steamship Historical Society Collection—Langsdale Library of the University of Baltimore, 1420 Maryland Ave., Baltimore, MD 21201; ph: 410-837-4334

Treasure Salvors, Inc.—200 Greene St., Key West, FL 33040; ph: 305-296-6533

United States Naval Historical Center—901 M St. SE, Washington Navy Yard, Washington, DC 20374-5060; web site: http://www.history.navy.mil

University of St. Andrews Archaeo-logical Diving Unit—St. Andrews, Fife KY16 9AJ United Kingdom; ph: +44-1334-462920; fax: +44-1334-462921; e-mail: io@st-andrews.ac.uk

SCUBA DIVING CERTIFICATION

Reading about a shipwreck only tells half the story. Seeing the wreck makes the tale come alive. Divers can explore wrecks around the world—in clear, blue tropical seas, in cooler local waters, and in many lakes and even some rivers. Wreck diving is one of the most popular specialty areas of scuba diving. The agencies listed here are among those that can provide information on obtaining scuba diving certification and the special training necessary to dive in and around shipwrecks.

American Canadian Underwater Certification (ACUC)— 1264 Osprey Drive, Ancaster, Ontario L9G 3L2 Canada; ph: 905-648-5500; fax: 905-648-5540; e-mail: acuc@acuc.ca

American Nitrox Divers International (ANDI)—74 Woodcleft Ave., Freeport, NY 11520; ph: 516-546-2026; fax: 516-546-6010

British Sub-Aqua Club (BSAC)— Telford's Quay, Ellesmere Port, South Wirral, Cheshire L65 4FY United Kingdom; ph: +44-151-357-1951; fax: +44-151-357-1250

Confederation Mondiale des Activités Subaquatiques (CMAS), also called World Underwater Federation— Viale Tisiano 74, Roma 00196 Italy; ph: +39-636858480; fax: +39-636858490

Handicapped Scuba Association International (HSA)—1104 El Prado, San Clemente, CA 92672-4637; ph/fax: 714-498-6128; e-mail: livelys@sprynet.com

International Association for Handicapped Divers (IAHD)— Box 1076, S-269 21 Båstad, Sweden; ph: +46-0431-69260; fax: +46-0431-69270; e-mail iadh@bastad.se

International Association of Nitrox and Technical Divers (IANTD)— 9628 NE Second Ave., Suite D, Miami Shores, FL 33138-2767; ph: 305-751-4873; fax: 305-751-3958; e-mail: iandthq@ix.netcom.com

International Diving Educators Association (IDEA)— P.O. Box 8427, Jacksonville, FL 32239; ph: 904-744-5554; fax: 904-743-5425; e-mail ideahq@aol.com

Japan Underwater Leaders & Instructors Association— Let's Bld 1F 2-18-5, Kohama-Nishi Suminoe-Ku, Osaka 559, Japan; ph: +816-675-1228; fax: +816-675-1229

Korea Underwater Association— Rm. 149, #2 Gymnasium, Oryun-dong, Songpa-ku, Seoul 138-151, Korea; ph: +822-420-4293; fax: +822-421-8898

Los Angeles County Underwater Association—419 E. 192nd St., Carson, CA 90745; ph: 213-327-5311

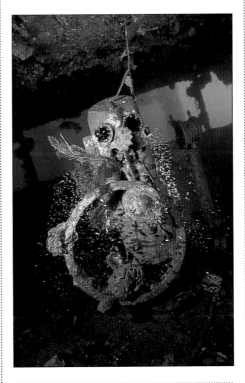

Taking journeys back in history, divers can visit the areas where sailors once worked, such as this helm from the *Nippo Maru*, covered with colorful sealife.

Multinational Diving Educators Association (MDEA)—244 Overseas Hwy., P.O. Box 523433, Marathon Shores, FL 33052; ph: 305-743-6188; fax: 305-743-7499

National Association of Scuba Educators (NASE)—1728 Kingsley Ave., Suite 6, Orange Park, FL 32073; ph: 904-264-4104; fax: 904-269-2283; e-mail: nasescuba@ilnk.com

National Association of Scuba Diving Schools (NASDS)—1012 S. Yates, Memphis, TN 38119; ph: 800-735-3483 or 901-767-7265; fax: 901-767-2798

National Association of Underwater Instructors (NAUI)—4650 Arrow Hwy. Suite F-1, Montclair, CA 91763; ph: 800-553-6284 or 909-621-5801; fax: 909-621-6405

PADI Wordwide—1251 E. Dyer Rd., #100, Santa Ana, CA 92705; ph: 800-792-7234 or 714-540-7234; fax: 714-540-2609

Professional Diving Instructors Corporation (PDIC) International— 1554 Gardner Ave., Scranton, PA 18509; ph: 717-342-1480; fax: 717-342-1276

Professional Scuba Association— 9480 NW 115 Ave., Ocala, FL 34482; ph: 407-896-6294; fax: 407-896-4542

Scuba Schools International (SSI)— 2619 Canton Court, Fort Collins, CO 80525-4498; ph: 800-821-4319 or 970-482-0883; fax: 970-482-6157; e-mail: admin@ssi-intl.com

Technical Diving International (TDI)— 9 Coastal Plaza, Suite 300, Bath, ME 04530; ph: 207-442-8391; fax: 207-442-9042

YMCA National Scuba Program— 5825-2A Live Oak Pkwy., Norcross, GA 30093; ph: 770-662-5172; fax: 770-242-9059; e-mail: scubaymca@aol.com

BIBLIOGRAPHY

FOR FURTHER READING

Alexander, Christopher, Gary Black, and Miyoko Tsutsui. *The Mary Rose Museum*. New York: Oxford University Press, 1995.

Amadon, George F. *Rise of the Ironclads*. Missoula, MT: Pictorial Histories Publishing Co., 1988.

Bailey, Dan E. *WWII Wrecks of the Kwajalein and Truk Lagoons*. Redding, CA: North Valley Diver Publications, 1989.

Ballard, Robert D. *The Discovery of the Titanic*. Toronto, Ont.: Warner/ Madison Press Books, 1989.

Bass, George F. *Ships and Shipwrecks of the Americas: A History Based on Underwater Archaeology*. New York: Thames and Hudson, Inc., 1988.

——. *Archaeology Beneath the Sea*. New York: Walker, 1975.

Bellico, Russell P. *Sails and Steam in the Mountains*. New York: Purple Mountain Press, 1992.

Berg, Daniel and Denise. *Tropical Shipwrecks*. East Rockaway, NY: Aqua Explorers Inc., 1989.

——. *Florida Shipwrecks*. East Rockaway, NY: Aqua Explorers Inc., 1991.

Biel, Steven. *Down with the Old Canoe: A Cultural History of the Titanic*. New York: W.W. Norton & Co., 1996.

Bohlander, Richard, ed. *World Explorers and Discoverers*. New York: Macmillan, 1992.

Bradford, Ernie. *The Story of the Mary Rose*. New York: W.W. Norton & Co., 1982.

Burgess, Robert F. *Sinkings, Salvages, and Shipwrecks*. New York: American Heritage Press, 1970.

Cafiero, Gaetano. *Sunken Treasures: The World's Greatest Shipwrecks*. Charlottesville, VA: Thomasson-Grant Inc., 1993

Conrad, Judy, ed. *Story of an American Tragedy: Survivors' Accounts of the Sinking of the Steamship Central America*. Columbus, OH: Columbus America Discovery Group, 1988.

Ferguson, David M., ed. *The Wrecks of Scapa Flow*. Stromness, Scotland: The Orkney Press, 1985.

Gentile, Gary. *Andrea Doria: Dive to an Era*. Philadelphia: Gary Gentile Productions, 1989.

——. *Shipwrecks of Delaware and Maryland*. Philadelphia: Gary Gentile Productions, 1990.

——. *Shipwrecks of New Jersey*. Norwalk, CT: Sea Sports Publications, 1988.

——. *Shipwrecks of North Carolina from Hatteras Inlet South*. Philadelphia: Gary Gentile Productions, 1992.

——. *Shipwrecks of Virginia*. Philadelphia: Gary Gentile Productions, 1992.

——. *U.S.S. San Diego: The Last Armored Cruiser*. Philadelphia: Gary Gentile Productions, 1989.

Hemming, Robert J. *Gales of November: the Sinking of the Edmund Fitzgerald*. Chicago: Contemporary Books, 1981.

Hendrickson, Robert, ed. *The Ocean Almanac*. New York: Doubleday, 1984.

Hoeling, Adolph A. *Thunder at Hampton Roads*. Englewood Cliffs, NJ: Prentice-Hall, 1976.

Hoeling, Adolph A. and Mary. *The Last Voyage of the Lusitania*. New York: Bonanza Books, 1991.

Hoffer, William. *Saved!* New York: Bantam Books, 1980.

Keatts, Henry C. and George C. Farrar. *Dive Into History Volume 1: Warships*. Houston: Pisces Books, 1990.

——. *Dive Into History Volume 2: U.S. Submarines*. Houston: Pisces Books, 1991.

——. *Dive Into History Volume 3: U-Boats*. Houston: Pisces Books, 1994.

Lindemann, Klaus P. *Hailstorm Over Truk Lagoon*. Singapore: Maruszen Asia Pte. Ltd, 1982

Lord, Walter. *A Night to Remember*. New York: Bantam Books [1988] © 1955.

Lyon, Eugene. *The Search for the Atocha*. New York: Harper & Row, 1979.

Marler, George and Luana. *The Royal Mail Steamer Rhone*. Tortola, BVI: High Tech Caribbean Ltd., 1978.

Marx, Robert and Jenifer. *New World Shipwrecks 1492–1925: A Comprehensive Guide*. Dallas: RAM Publishing Company, 1994

Marx, Robert F. *The Search for Sunken Treasure: Exploring the World's Great Shipwrecks*. Toronto, Ontario: Key Porter Books, 1993.

Mathewson, R. Duncan III. *Treasure of the Atocha*. New York: Dutton, 1986.

Matthews, Rupert. *The Attack on the Lusitania*. New York: Bookwright Press, 1989.

McKee, Alexander. *King Henry VIII's Mary Rose*. New York: Stein and Day, 1974.

Mokin, Arthur. *Ironclad: The Monitor and the Merrimack*. Novato, CA: Presidio, 1991.

Moscow, Alvin. *Collision Course: the Andrea Doria and the Stockholm*. New York: Putnam, 1959.

Sheard, Bradley. *Beyond Sportdiving: Exploring the Deepwater Shipwrecks of the Atlantic*. Birmingham, AL: Menasha Ridge Press, 1991.

Skerry, Brian and Henry Keatts. *Complete Wreck Diving*. San Diego: Watersport Publishing, Inc., 1995

Snyder, Gerald S. *The Royal Oak Disaster*. San Rafael, CA: Presidio Press, [1978] © 1976.

Stick, David. *Graveyard of the Atlantic*. Chapel Hill, NC: University of North Carolina Press, 1952.

Zarzynski, Joseph W. *Monster Wrecks of Loch Ness and Lake Champlain*. Wilton, NY: M-Z Information, 1986.

A

Abbass, D.K., 30
Abercromby, James, 31
Admiralty Law, 26
Aikoku Maru (transport ship), 91
Alcoa Seaprobe (salvage ship), 50
Anderson, Elga, 106
Andrea Doria (liner), 9, 50, 100, *100–101,*
    101, 102, *102–103,* 103, 104, *104,*
    106, 107
Arctic Discoverer (salvage ship), 40
Armaments, 19, 20, 23, 24, *24,* 29, 34, 42, 45,
    53, *53*
Artifacts, 14, 15, 17, *17,* 20, 24, 39, *39. See
    also* Treasure
   Bronze Age, 17, *17*
   Byzantine, 17, *17*
   personal, 19, *19,* 20, 38, *38*
Astor, John Jacob, 59
Atlantis II, 64

B

Bahamas, 26
Ballard, Robert, 63, 64, 75, 96
Bartram, Evelyn, 106
Bass, George, 6, 14, 15
Bateaux Below, Inc., 29, 30
Bellico, Russell, 30
Bemis, F. Gregg Jr., 75
Bends. *See* Decompression
Benway, Bob, 30
Bielenda, Steve, 106
Bligh, William, 32, 33, *33,* 34, *34*
Bozburun (Turkey), 15
British Virgin Islands, 52, 53, 55, 56
Brummer (cruiser), 81
Bryan, William Jennings, 72

C

Çakir, Mehmet, 12
Calamai, Piero, 102, 103
Californian, 59, 60, 62
Campbell, Bill, 106
Capone, Vincent, 30
Caroline Islands, 85
Cembrola, Robert, 30
Charles (Prince of Wales), 18, 20
Christian, Fletcher, 32
Churchill, Winston, 83
Columbus-America Discovery Group, Inc.,
    39, 40, 41
Conservation, 20, *20,* 21
Cousteau, Jacques, 49, 50
Crete, 15
Cropp, Ben, 34
CSS *Virginia* (ironclad), 42–46
Cyprus, 14

D

Dauntless (salvage vessel), 22
Deane, John and Charles, 20
Decompression, 14

Denlay, Kevin, 96
Dolan, Hugh, 50
Domm, Steve, 34
Dor (Israel), 15
Dresden (cruiser), 81
Dudas, John, 106
Dumas, Frederic, 104

E

Edgerton, Harold "Doc," 20
Edmund Fitzgerald (ore carrier), 108, *108,* 109,
    110, 111–113
Edwards, Edward, 33
Ellen (bark), 39
Empress of Ireland, 62
Equipment
   aerial magnetometers, 27
   air systems, 14
   Aqua-Lungs, 74
   diving helmets, 20
   magnetometers, 24, 34
   respirators, 20, *20*
Ericsson, John, 42, 43
Evans, Robert, 39
Exploration and salvage, *13, 15, 16, 23, 23*
   Acoustically Navigated Geological
      Underwater Survey, 63, 64
   and Admiralty Law, 26
   Andrea Doria, 9, 50, 100–107
   Central America, 36–41
   computers in, 39
   diver propulsion vehicles in, 49
   Edmund Fitzgerald, 108–113
   fittings, 21, *21*
   funding, 23
   galleons, 22–27
   Land Tortoise, 28, 28, 29, *29,* 30, *30,* 31
   lawsuits over, 23–24, 41, 75
   leases, 26, 27
   Lusitania (liner), 70–75
   Mary Rose, 19–21
   Mediterranean, 12–17
   methods, 24
   Monitor, 45–51
   Nuestra Señora de Atocha, 6, 22–25
   Pandora, 32–34
   remotely operated vehicles in, 40
   Rhone, 6, 52–57
   robots, 64, 66
   submersibles in, 49, 64
   television in, 49
   Titanic, 58–69
   videography in, 30, 40
Explorers' Club, 29

F

Farb, Ron, 50
Fisher, Angel, 24
Fisher, Dirk, 24
Fisher, Mel, 6, 22, 23, 24, 25, 26
Florida Keys National Marine Sanctuary, 24
Fort Pierce Bay (Florida), 26
Fox, Joseph, 100
France, 18

Freiderich der Grosse (warship), 79–80
Fujikawa Maru (transport ship), 86, 87

G

Gage, Rick, 24
Gambone, Guido, 107
Gatto, Steve, 106
Gentile, Gary, 49, 50, 75
Giddings, Al, 88
Gimbel, Peter, 6, 100, 104, 106
Great Barrier Reef (Australia), 34
Grimm, Jack, 41, 63
Guggenheim, Benjamin, 59, 61

H

Haisman, Edith, 68
Halsey, William "Bull," 99
Hampton Roads (Virginia), 42, 43, 45, 46
Havana (Cuba), 22, 26
Henry VIII (King of England), 18
Hernson, William Lewis, 37, *37,* 38, 39
Hess, Peter, 50
HMS *Abercrombie* (warship), 83
HMS *Bounty* (frigate), 32, 33, *33,* 34, 35
HMS *Hampshire* (warship), 78, 79, *79*
HMS *Pandora* (frigate), 32–34
HMS *Roberts* (warship), 83
HMS *Royal Oak* (warship), 80, 81, 82, 83, *83*
Horan, David Paul, 23

I

International Convention for Safety of Life
    at Sea, 62
Inverlane (tanker), 78, *78*
Ismay, J. Bruce, 59

J

James, Chris, 26
Jason Junior (robot), 64, 66
John, Harry G., 41

K

Karlsruhe (cruiser), 81
Kellam, Richard B., 41
Key West (Florida), 22
Kilabuk (salvage ship), 68
Knorr (salvage ship), 63
Koga, Mineichi, 87
Köln (cruiser), 81
König (battleship), 81
Kronprinz Wilhelm (battleship), 81

L

Lake George (New York), 6, 29–31
Land Tortoise (radeau), 6, *28, 28,* 29, *29,* 30,
    30, 31
Lane, Hugh, 73
Le Suroit (salvage ship), 63
Light, John, 74, 75
Lord, Walter, 104

Lusitania (liner), 70, *70*, 71, *71*, 72, 73, *73*, 74, *74*, 75
Lyon, Eugene, 23

M

"Mad Mac's Marauders," 20
Magnetometers, 24, 34
  aerial, 27
Malle, Louis, 104
Maple Leaf (warship), 31
Marden, Luis, 32
Marine Archaeological Research Ltd., 27
Marine (brig), 37, 38
Markgraf (battleship), 81
Mary Rose (warship), 18, *18*, 19, 20, *20*, 21, *21*
Mathewson, R. Duncan III, 25, 31
Matroci, Andy, 25
McKee, Alexander, 20
McMahon, Kendrick, 30
Mediterranean Sea, 12–17
Merrimack. See CSS Virginia
Michel, Jean-Louis, 63
Molson, Harry, 59
Moyer, John, 106, 107
Musashi (battleship), 87, 88

N

Nadir (research ship), 68
Nagle, Bill, 106
Narcosis, 14
National Geographic Society, 32, 75
National Oceanic and Atmospheric
    Administration, 24, 49, 50
National Register of Historic Places, 31, 47
Nautile (submarine), 66, 68
Newton, John, 47
Nimitz, Chester, 85
Nippo Maru, 87, 88, 91
Norfolk (Virginia), 41
Northwind (tug), 24
Nuestra Señora de Atocha (galleon), 6, 22, *22*, 23–25
Nuestra Señora de las Maravillas (galleon), 26–27

O

Oceaneering International, 75
Operation Bateaux, 31
Operation Hailstorm, 85, 87, 92

P

Palestine, 14
Payne, Theodore, 37
Pearl Harbor (Hawaii), 9, 85, 92–94
Philip IV (King of Spain), 22
Pitcairn Island, 32
Portsmouth (England), 18, 19
Potter, John, 22
President Coolidge (liner), 96, *96*, 97, 98
Prien, Gunther, 79, *79*, 83
Pulak, Cemal, 12, *16*, 17

R

Raveh, Kurt, 17
Reuter, Ludwig von, 76, 78

RMS *Rhone*, 6, 52, 53, *53*, *54–55*, 55, 56, 57
RMS *Titanic* (liner), 58, 59–60, *61*, 61, 62–64, 65, *65*, 66, 68, *68*, 69
Robin (robot), 66
Royal Mail Steam Packet Company, 52
Rule, Margaret, 20 Π

S

Salvage. *See* Exploration and salvage
Santa Margarita (galleon), 22, 23, 24
Scapa Flow (Scotland), 6, 76–83
Schatz, Barry, 39
Schweiger, Karl, 71, 72
Seydlitz (warship), 80, *80*
Shinkoku Maru (warship), 84, 88
Shouppe, Stephen, 26
Sicily, 15
Smith, Edward, 59, 61, 65, *65*
Spruance, Raymond, 87
SS *Carpathia*, 62, 63, 64, 66, *66*, 67
SS *Central America* (steamship), 6, 36, *36–37*, 37, 38, *38*, 39, *39*, 40, *40*, 41
Stockholm, 101, *101*, 103–104, *105*
Straus, Ida, 59, 61
Straus, Isidor, 59
Submarines, German, 71, 83
Submerged Heritage Preserves, 31
Syria, 14

T

Tahiti, 33
Tantura Lagoon (Israel), 15, 17
Tapson, Polly, 75
Tequesta (galleon), 26
Thompson, Thomas, 39
Throckmorton, Peter, 14
Treasure, 6, 6, *12*, *13*, 14, 17, *17*, 23, 24, 25, *25*, 26, *26*, 27, *27*, 40, *40*, 41, *41*
Treasure Salvors, Inc., 22, 24
Tulloch, George, 66, 68
Turner, William, 71
Tysall, Terrence, 96

U

Uluburun (Turkey), 12, 14, 15
United States Navy, 24
USS *Arizona* (battleship), *8–9*, 9, 31, 92, *92*, 93, *93*, 94
USS *Bunker Hill* (carrier), 88
USS *Congress* (warship), 43
USS *Cumberland* (warship), 43
USS *Enterprise* (carrier), 88, 94
USS *Illinois* (supply ship), 72
USS *Minnesota* (warship), 44, 45
USS *Monitor* (ironclad), 9, 31, 42, 43, *43*, 44, *44*, 45, *45*, 46, *46*, 47, *47*, 48, 49, *49*, 50, 50, *51*
USS *New Jersey* (battleship), 87
USS *Rhode Island* (warship), 46, 47
USS *Utah* (battleship), 31
USS *Yorktown* (carrier), 88

W

Wachsmann, Shelley, 17
Wagner, Kip, 26

Wareham, Greg, 25
Wars, 9
    French and Indian, 29, 31
    War of 1812, 31, 78
    World War I, 70–75, 76–83
    World War II, 84–99
Weather, 9, 26, 36, 37, 53
Weller, Bob and Margaret, 26
White Star Line, 59, 62
Wilson, Woodrow, 72
Wooley, Robert, 52–53

Y

Yamagiri Maru (warship), 84, 88
Yamato (battleship), 88